DEVON'S CHURCHES

A Celebration

DEVON'S CHURCHES

A Celebration

John Lane

with photographs by

Harland Walshaw

Green Books

Dedication

To Peter Ashton, a devout Christian
and dear friend for more than sixty years.

Published in 2007
by Green Books, Foxhole, Dartington
Totnes, Devon TQ9 6EB

Designed by Rick Lawrence
rick@samskara-design.com

Captions not given in the text:
Front of jacket, Honeychurch; p1 Trumpeting angel on roof of Winkleigh church;
p2 Angel in porch at Dartington; p7 Green Man on pillar at East Budleigh;
p9 Elizabethan arms in Tavistock porch; p11 Carving on gallery, Kentisbeare;
p13 Commandment boards, Bratton Clovelly; p14 Painted organ, Ringmore;
p15 Window at Gittisham; p16 Buckland in the Moor; p17 Sign at High Bickington;
pp118-9 North aisle windows, Kenn; p120 Dowland; p121 Elizabethan communion rail,
Pilton; pp200-1 Screen at Kenton; p202 14th-century knight, Atherington; p203 Light
fitting, St Mary Abbotsbury, Newton Abbot; p245 Inscription by Harry Hems, Revelstoke.

Text printed and bound by TJ International Ltd, Padstow, Cornwall, UK
on 9lives 55 paper (55% recycled fibre, 45% virgin fibre from sustainable forests)

ISBN 978 1 903998 96 0

Contents

Author's
acknowledgements

I would like to acknowledge my debt to those who have contributed to this book. The first of these is my friend Harland Walshaw, with whom I travelled to many of the churches. The quality of his photographs will speak for itself, but Harland also advised on and edited my text in ways for which I am deeply grateful. The second person to whom both of us owe a tremendous debt is Peter Burton for his friendship, constant stimulation and valuable editing. Other people to whom I am grateful include Rosie Bowen, my indefatigable, patient and enthusiastic driver on several church crawls, and our publisher John Elford and his staff, for whom no trouble was ever too much. This enthusiasm, patience and expertise has been a constant and invaluable support. But first and foremost, I would like to thank my wife, Truda, for her continuous, unselfish and loving support. It is hard to express adequate gratitude.

In working on this book, I have relied on the help of many others including Patricia Alvis, Anne and Ron Atkin, the Rev. R. W. Bamberg, Antonia Barker, Annabel Beamney, the Rev. John Carvossa, Rebecca Child, Diane Collinson, David Fitter, the Venerable David Gunn-Johnson, David Halestrap, the Rev. Colin Hodgetts, Peter Howells, the Rev. Jeremy Hummerstone, the Rev. Nicola Hunt, Richard Keasing, Adrian Lunnon, Penny McRoberts, Graham Miller, Nathaniel Lane, Victoria Littlewood, Grania Luttman-Johnson, Pamela Macey, the Rev. Graham Mayer, Robert Potter, Terry Pincombe, Anne Primavesi, Robin Ravilious, Cyril Rider, Ralph Rochester, Mark Rylands, Bernard Samuels, Roger Thorne, the Rev. Stephen Thorpe, John and Hamish Turner, the Rev. David Ursell, Michael Wynne-Powell, and all those who so kindly responded to my note in the Diocesan News requesting suggestions about churches I might consider visiting. I would also like to thank Dr David Keep for so generously contributing the essay on Nonconformist architecture, and the staff of Torrington Public Library for their help with books.

Finally I should like to thank Phillimore & Co Ltd for permission to publish a passage from *Devon* by W. G. Hoskins (reprinted 2003).

Photographer's acknowledgements

Many people helped in various ways with the photography for this book, and were most generous with their time and advice. I particularly want to thank Suki Commin, Jo Cox, Richard Crisp, Helen Dimond, Anna Lunk, Jocelyn Morris, Dennis Pickering, Peter Reid, Ralph Rochester, John Welton and Clive Wilson, as well as all the vicars and churchwardens who have opened up their churches and allowed me to take photographs.

Liz and Hester Walshaw, my wife and daughter, have both given me an enormous amount of help, in spite of having to endure my obsession with churches for over a year.

Ken Carter, sculptor (1928-2007), was a constant source of encouragement. Visiting a church with him helped to open my eyes, and I learned a great deal about the monuments in particular from his professional expertise. He loved to look at the photographs, and I am sad that he did not live to see the book.

Peter Burton has been my photographic mentor and partner for many years. He has developed the films, given me the run of his darkroom, and helped with all the printing that is involved in taking black-and-white photographs with such an old-fashioned, wonderful camera as my Rolleiflex.

Introduction

This book arises from a lifelong pleasure in the churches of England, and more particularly from a forty-year acquaintance with the churches of Devon. It is a celebration of all that is most inspiring, imaginative and beautiful in the long history of the county's ecclesiastical architecture, an exploration of its finest churches and their architecture and fittings, and of the centrality and beauty of Christian ritual in country life.

In the course of its writing I and my collaborator, Harland Walshaw, whose photographs are central to the book, undertook the task of visiting more than 200 buildings – a kind of pilgrimage – in the course of a single year. We might have visited all of the county's 624 churches, but time and money are not bottomless, and the full complement would have made this an unwieldy and expensive volume. It is therefore inevitable that some will find certain much-loved churches have regrettably been left out.

In this search we travelled to every part of the county: from the tiny church of Trentishoe on the remote fringes of untamed Exmoor to Branscombe on the south coast, from Welcombe facing the Atlantic breakers to Holcombe Rogus close to Somerset. We travelled across open moorland, along deep banked lanes, through hidden valleys, little villages and several market towns. We experienced rain and sunshine, frosted landscapes and fields dazzling with fresh-grown grass. At one time the hedgerows shone with clumps of primroses, at another there were fieldfares, rushing streams and wintry, nut-coloured woods. In every case our destination was a sacred building whose pursuit took us into a countryside more ravishing than anyone can reasonably expect to find. If some of Devon has been spoiled by ugliness, drab uniformity and cheerless impersonality, to this day the bulk remains superb. Those of us who were born or who have settled here must count it our good fortune that we live in one of the most beautiful regions of the world.

We might also rejoice in the existence of these parish churches. We hope this book, its descriptions and pictures, will convey at least some of the mood of exultation we enjoyed when we walked up their churchyard paths, passed through their ancient porches, pushed open their heavy doors, gazed at their interiors and recognised yet again a great work of imagination. Where else could one expect to find what they offer, and in such prodigious numbers? For us it has been a constant source of wonder to visit these shining treasures almost any day of the week.

In memory they are all poetry, intimacy, prayer. They are reminders of our predecessors' quest for the earthly expression of the eternal and, no less, for the resplendence of the Christian rural culture, which for centuries nourished the people of this land. When I recall the great panorama of the county's churches – Ashton with its ancient granite arcade, Babbacombe with its sumptuous, dusky interior, Cullompton with the Handelian splendour of its decorated roof and Talaton with its heroic tower, I begin to experience something as richly lyrical, honest and visionary as the sonnets of Shakespeare, the masses of Byrd and the watercolours of John Sell Cotman. But that is not all. There is the luxurious splendour of Devon's many glorious rood-screens, the unsophisticated rusticity of churches such as Buckland in the Moor, Molland and Hittisleigh, and the many fonts as vigorous and munificent as hedgerow haws.

Over the years I have had the good fortune to visit some of the finest buildings in the world – most of the great French Romanesque and Gothic cathedrals, the buildings of Brunelleschi, Angkor Wat in Cambodia, Tanjore and the Taj Mahal in India, the mosques of Isfahan and Istanbul's Hagia Sophia, as well as the temples of Japan. It is obvious that apart from Exeter's great cathedral not one of the county's churches can compare with any of these. But when we look at them as a whole, when we regard them as an integral element within the Devon landscape, it is a different story – an exultant celebration of the richness of spirit of a traditional civilisation, at once glorious, modest and joyful. This book is a hymn to these buildings and to the men and women who built and continue to care for them.

John Lane
Beaford

How the churches were chosen

I knew some that had to be included, churches which I had loved for decades: Honeychurch, Parracombe, Kings Nympton and Hartland. Then there were those I had discovered during the preparation of an earlier book, *In Praise of Devon: A Guide to its People, Places and Character*: West Ogwell, Ottery St Mary, Dittisham, and St Saviour's in Dartmouth. But in the preparation of this volume I travelled into even remoter parts.

I turned first to the many churches – just over a hundred – whose descriptions were provided by W. G. Hoskins for John Betjeman's *Collins Guide to English Parish Churches*, first published in 1958. To my mind, Hoskins is a most reliable guide to churches earlier than the Victorian period, whose judgement can usually be trusted. This is especially so when his choice is backed up by Alec Clifton-Taylor, who provides his own list in *English Churches as Works of Art* (1974). And then, of course, there is Nikolaus Pevsner's and Bridget Cherry's *Devon* in *The Buildings of England* series (1991). As a piece of scholarship, the Pevsner is a glorious achievement, and one for which all those delighted by architecture must feel nothing but admiration. However, it deliberately avoids subjective judgements, which makes it sometimes difficult to decide which churches are most worth visiting. I therefore judged that a guide which included qualitative descriptions of the feel or atmosphere of the finest Devon churches would be a useful complement to his work. This is something which Simon Jenkins does extremely well in his study of *England's Thousand Best Churches* (1999), but alas it only includes 33 in Devon. Ann Jellicoe's descriptions in *The Devon Shell Guide* of 1975 are both perceptive and brilliantly written, with many a telling phrase, but necessarily brief. A study of those listed by English Heritage as Grade I (229 in Devon) led me to discover a few more, although sometimes it seems that age alone ensures a listing.

And then there were personal recommendations. Take, for example, the church in Farringdon (see page 147), which lies some distance from where I live. Should it be visited? Hoskins in his wonderful book, *Devon*, describes the decorated brick interior as "hideous". Ann Jellicoe writes, "Church restored 1871 with Art Nouveau designs painted directly on to bare brickwork". Pevsner reports non-committedly, "Interior faced with red brick, stencilled. N arcade of purple Trap with Ham Hill shafts. Rere-arches to all the windows. Simple fittings." It did not make our list. But then a friend said, "Have you been to Farringdon? It's just the kind of church that anyone would want in their village." We were not disappointed. Farringdon may not be comparable to, say, Plymtree, Torbryan or even Eggesford, but it's a place of delight nonetheless, a church that others should be encouraged to see.

Our choice is, of course, personal and no doubt prejudiced. We have reluctantly left out many churches we only partially admired, and have chosen some that others might not have included. So if a church you love is not here, I apologise for its omission. Nonetheless, do not be deterred from seeking out an unknown church simply because it is not in this guide. But we can promise you that all the churches that *are* included are worth a visit. When John Betjeman and John Piper were preparing the *Collins Guide to English Parish Churches*, they spent many hours discussing whether churches were 'winners' or 'too dim' for inclusion. All the churches you will find in these pages are winners.

Access to churches

In the course of our travels, we were thrilled to find how many of Devon's churches were open during daylight hours (and a few even for 24 hours each day). When Henry Thorold revisited the churches of Lincolnshire 20 years ago, it was a different picture: "It has been gloomy work because so many churches are now kept locked. Is this necessary? It is not. Even in these pagan days, these days of progress and vandalism, churches should be open – valuables, if necessary, stowed away. This, after all, is what they were built for. A locked church forfeits the prayers of the faithful: it also forfeits the offerings of visitors. It is a church in retreat." (*Lincolnshire Churches Revisited*, published by Michael Russell.) Clearly the church in Devon is not in retreat, but even so the unwary visitor will find some churches locked. Our invaluable handbook was the annual *Exeter Diocesan Directory*, which gives the phone numbers of all the clergy and churchwardens. They were invariably helpful, supportive of the idea of the book, and if their church was locked were willing to open it for us. Talking to them was one of the pleasures of our work. If you are keen to see a particular church, do phone up first.

Why we visit churches

"An ancient and beautiful church fulfils its primary function merely by existing. It is, in itself, and irrespective of the numbers using it, an act of worship. A beautiful church, whether standing alone in the countryside, or surrounded by wharves and warehouses, offices and houses, is a perpetual reminder of spiritual values. In Shakespeare's phrase, such churches are 'sermons in stones', and their message is delivered not for half an hour on Sundays, but every hour of every day of every year; and not merely to those who enter, but to all who pass by. It is only in modern times that the belief has arisen that a church has to be filled regularly with worshippers to justify its existence."

from a Memorandum published by The Friends of Friendless Churches

Whether or not we subscribe to the faith of their creators, churches and other places of worship – nonconformist chapels, Quaker meeting houses, synagogues, cathedrals – though originally built as shelters in which the faithful could pray and worship, continue to retain a place in our hearts and a hold on our imagination. Why is this so? Christians, of course, go to celebrate their faith and worship their God, in the presence of fellow believers; to marry, to baptise and to bury. But why do agnostics, atheists, humanists and secularists, as well as those who are just looking for somewhere to go on their day off, find sacred buildings not only interesting but often deeply moving? Why, as church-going declines, does church-visiting increase? There is, of course, more than one reason.

Some visit out of curiosity. Some out of a love of architecture and to admire the strange and wondrous treasures within. Some to enjoy tranquillity and enter a different age where time stands still and traditions are still potent. Some for more personal reasons. "Came to see where great, great, great grandparents got married," someone has written in the visitors' book of Down St Mary.

There is yet another attraction: the lure of the historic past. The very fabric of a church tells us of mercantile ambition and economic depression, plague and prosperity, the rise and fall of populations, the growth and decay of the ideas which have guided our history. What other building embodies the collective memory of its community's past? What other building speaks so eloquently of memories and fellowship?

The author of the guidebook to the church of Lew Trenchard, Bickford H. C. Dickinson (whom I slightly knew), suggests a further reason why churches are being visited. It is, he suggests, our unacknowledged need to discover and pay tribute to our English roots.

"There is a quiet here," he writes, "broken only by the song of the birds and the hum of the bees in the great lime trees. Here we can pause for a while, and feel about us for a nostalgic moment something of that older, more peaceful England, whose rhythms were based on the eternal things; on sunrise and sunset, on seed time and harvest; that rural England that the younger generation has never known and which it becomes harder yearly for us older ones to recall, but which Sabine [Baring-Gould] loved and understood so much."

There is, perhaps, a deeper, if unconscious, attraction. I suspect that people visit churches because they are looking to find some kind of refreshment, some kind of heart's ease, a breathing space for their beleaguered spirits. The church visit, however brief, has this importance: it offers at least the possibility of a transitory escape, a still haven, a place of retreat from the hustle and bustle of everyday existence. Where modern life is overwhelmingly secular, it offers a sense of the sacred; where it is transitory, a sense of stability and permanence; where it is ugly, a vision of the beautiful; and where it is individualistic, a sense of communality. In exchange for the noise and restlessness of the world, it provides the serenity of silence, the solace of calm, a haven for contemplation.

O PRAY·FOR·THE·PEACE·OF·JERUSALEM

FIFTY
SELECTED
CHURCHES

ASHTON
St John the Baptist

3m/4km N of Chudleigh

Set high on a rocky eminence in the luxuriant countryside of the western slopes of Haldon, this Perpendicular church, entirely rebuilt and refurnished between 1400 and 1485, is a singularly beautiful building. It has a harmonious and well proportioned interior shaped out of local materials – granite windows, columns of Beer stone, bare flagstone floors and plain, buff-coloured plaster – which on the morning of my visit were bathed in light from its clear glass windows. A sparse yet elegant rusticity is the keynote of this wonderful interior.

The attractive rood-screen and loft, with three bands of cornice decoration, has some of the best panel painting in Devon: 32 figures of saints and doctors of the church in its frontal wainscot and several larger prophets (which could have been based on contemporary woodcuts) on the back of the screen, that is within the former Chudleigh family chapel. These have wonderful ribbons of lettering surrounding each painted figure.

The tracery of the screen is individual, with shapes and signs of the original colouring. There are also carved mediaeval bench ends, some stained glass, including figures of Gabriel and St Sidwell with a scythe, a handsome Jacobean pulpit with a sounding board, a set of seventeenth-century altar rails, and on the south wall a faded mural of Christ with the instruments of His Passion. There is not an ounce of pretension or show in this still and deeply peaceful place.

Above left: Ledger stone.
Facing page: The Angel Gabriel on the back of the screen.

ATHERINGTON

St Mary

7m/11km S of Barnstaple

The tall, somewhat military tower commands large views of the high, sweeping north Devon landscape as far as Exmoor. It is situated on a hilltop, and is a landmark for miles.

The predominantly fifteenth- and sixteenth-century interior has a friendly rustic character, but is chiefly memorable because of its contents, especially its wonderful rood-loft across the short north aisle, unique in Devon. It has branching tracery, Early Renaissance motifs (putti for example) and a rich cornice of energetic vegetation. This was the work of three local carvers, one of whom, John Pares or Parrys, "Kyrver" of Northlew, began the screen, which was apparently completed by two new craftsmen, Roger Down and John Hyll, "carpenters, carvers, and joiners" from nearby Chittlehampton between 1533 and 1547.

Although more numerous in the West Country than anywhere else in England, surviving examples of this short-lived Early Renaissance style, in which traditional and Renaissance motifs are satisfactorily blended together, are rare.

Other features in the church include, in the north aisle, a complete window of mediaeval glass made up by Clayton and Bell (1883), and a sensitive but much eroded thirteenth-century carving of a recumbent knight, one of the earliest in the country with crossed legs, perhaps Sir William de Champernowne (see page 203). There is also a monument to two fourteenth-century figures said to be of Sir Ralph Wylmington, Kt. and Lady Eleanor (Mohun). On the

other side of the church is a transept with a simple but lovely wagon roof. On its west wall is a handsome memorial for Anthony Snell, yeoman, d.1707.

The church was restored in 1882-1900 by J. L. Pearson, one of the most sensitive of Victorian restorers, who left the Devonian tracery when he renewed the windows. In 1884 a lychgate was added and in 1953 a new altar and reredos, both, alas, unworthy to stand alongside the great sixteenth-century screen whose unassuming poetry puts them to shame.

Above: The rood-loft.
Facing page: Putti on screen tracery.

BABBACOMBE
All Saints

A suburb of Torquay

William Butterfield's church of All Saints in Babbacombe would not come high on most people's list of great buildings, but for me it is a masterpiece. I enjoy its intensity of religious fervour and moral rectitude, its ferocious confidence and tightly controlled architectural invention.

It was built between 1865 and 1867 (east end and tower 1872-4) to serve the expanding population of Torquay, and remains surrounded by villas and rows of houses from which its great stern tower and spire rise up with a thrilling assertiveness.

The sumptuous richness of the interior is at once powerful, mystical, even gloomy, yet with a surprising element of sensuous delight. Polished drums of Devon marble in two shades of brown uphold the nave's red and grey sandstone walls, which are decorated with an insistent and irregular chequer pattern. The cambered roof with its quatrefoil clerestory windows adds a further sombre note of umber. It is however the lighter-coloured chancel with its brightly coloured east window, representing God in Majesty surrounded by the Elders in Heavenly Worship (designed by Alexander Gibbs in 1874), which attracts attention. Here the polychrome treatment of the walls is continued and there are tightly disciplined but almost athletic architectural features, described by one critic, Goodhart-Rendel, as "of an inspired strangeness". The chancel floor is a wonderful composition of different marbles: pinks, grey-blues and buffs, with highlights of black, sea-green and veined yellow. An even more inventive employment of different marbles is to be found in the font and ceremonial pulpit. These must be amongst the most spectacular versions of their kind in England.

Butterfield built for the glory of God. All Saints can be accused of hardness and severity, but these, like his honesty and courage, were born of his faith. In that, as in so much else, this stern Christian followed the path of his mediaeval predecessors.

Above: Chancel windows.
Facing page: The chancel.

BERE FERRERS
St Andrew

7m/11km S of Tavistock

On the morning of our visit the broad lake-like river shone beneath a great burning-glass of sky. Curlews called, and the silent church, situated on a remote tongue of land close to the meeting of the Tavy and Tamar, felt completely isolated from the surrounding human world. With the tide lapping the churchyard, this church has one of the most striking settings of any in Devon.

Yet the exterior, sadly rendered with a grey coat of cement, is rather unprepossessing. In contrast the interior, largely built by Sir William de Ferrers in *c.*1330-33 (and therefore belonging to a period earlier than nearly all the other churches in south Devon) is deeply attractive. It consists of a nave, long transept, and chancel, plus a south aisle and south transept. There are fine granite arcades, whitewashed walls and a series of windows dating from several periods. Overall the church is characterised by a poetic quality at once light and serene.

Special features include the vigorously carved Hardwick stone Norman font, and in the east window some beautiful early fourteenth-century glass reassembled from broken fragments, magically coloured in royal blues, deep yellow ochres, smoky whites, and a pane of surprising tomato red. In the chancel there is an unusually sensitive monument of a cross-legged knight and a lady wearing a wimple, set in a tomb recess. The tomb's white limestone Decorated-style canopy is ornamented at the ends of the cusps with delicate heads and with exquisitely carved censing angels in the gables. Another Ferrers monument of a cross-legged knight is in the north aisle. There are a number of carved bench ends in the nave, three piscinas, and in the crowded churchyard which overlooks the river, several eighteenth-century slate tablets. The most poignant records a simple cry of pain: "Cholera 1849".

Above: Details of angel heads on tomb in chancel.
Facing page: North transept with effigy of cross-legged knight in recess.

BERRY POMEROY

St Mary

2m/3km E of Totnes

This late fifteenth-century church with its large, stately, Perpendicular windows and powerful tower sits beautifully in the churchyard of dark and spreading yews.

Open the door and you are faced with the full glory of a great rich Devonshire screen. It crosses the width of the building from the north to the south wall, and its coving, cornice and cresting have been preserved intact (see page 225). There is much original work and the gleam of gold. The screen's exceptionally vigorous carving of verdant, branching stem and flower dominates the otherwise relative austerity of the interior of this church.

But there are also good bosses and in addition two delightful monuments, one to Sir Richard Pomeroy of 1496 and another to the Seymour family of 1613. The latter consists of three stiff full-length bodies lying above and slightly behind one another: Lord Edward and Sir Edward and his wife and family are propped on their elbows in poses reminiscent of early Buddhist sculpture, but unintentionally funnier. The children are tenderly represented: one in a cot, another facing outwards in a chair, and a group of others in deep relief, kneeling in prayer.

Facing page: The Seymour family tomb.

BICTON
The Rolle Mausoleum

3m/4km N of Budleigh Salterton

A romantic site on the perimeter of the grounds of Bicton House comprises no less than three ecclesiastical buildings: the roofless, John Piperish ruin of the mediaeval church of Holy Trinity, the nineteenth-century church of St Mary's in the Decorated style by John Hayward (accomplished but dull), and in the south chancel of the original church, a chapel, the Rolle mausoleum of 1849-50. This may look nothing special, but inside it is an astonishing surprise.

It amazes for two reasons. First, the Baroque tomb of Denys Rolle (died *c.*1638), which consists of two life-size figures, is superb. His wife is recumbent, he reclining, propped up on his elbow on a tomb-chest. Beneath, at floor level, there is the tenderest representation of a sleeping child. The authorship of this exquisite work remains uncertain – attributions include both William Wright and Nicholas Stone – but whoever it was, he was certainly a master of exceptional accomplishment.

But secondly, this mortuary chapel for Lord John Rolle (who died in 1842) is a fascinating example of the work of the apostle of Gothic principles, the architect and theorist A. W. N. Pugin. There is an ornate floor tiled by Minton, two stained-glass windows by Hardman, a

high vaulted roof painted with formal and heraldic patterns, and against the north wall the intricately carved Rolle monument, sculpted by George Myers, but of course to Pugin's designs.

The day on which we visited was strongly atmospheric of romantic feudalism. The ruined church and the mortuary chapel, backed by a wintry wood of damp, ivy-clad trees, was the epitome of melancholy. The deep carpet of fallen beech leaves silenced our footsteps.

Above: Sleeping child at the foot of the tomb of Denys Rolle, 1638.
Facing page: The Rolle monument.

BOVEY TRACEY

St Peter, St Paul & St Thomas of Canterbury

5m/8km NW of Newton Abbot

Largely of the fifteenth century with a tall, tapering and sensitive fourteenth-century tower, the church has a spacious interior and five-bay nave arcades of Beer stone with delicately carved capitals. The unplastered wooden roof over the sanctuary has forty carved unpainted bosses of foliate designs (see page 228) and two grinning heads. But it is the superb eleven-bay rood-screen which captures the attention. With its richly carved cornice frieze, leaf scrolls, birds, foliage and fruit, it is of an exceptional quality. Said to date from 1427, it was restored in 1887-8 when most of the colour was added. However, the paintings on its wainscot of Apostles and Prophets are original (see page 224). The Parclose side screens were made in the sixteenth century, and the stone pulpit, brass eagle lectern of East Anglian origin and font originated in the fifteenth century.

In the chancel are two Jacobean monuments. That to Nicholas Eveleigh is especially extravagant; he died in 1618, aged 56, when the roof of the Stannary Court House at Chagford fell in and killed him and nine others. This monument was erected by his wife, Alice Bray, and shows her husband in armour, carved in white stone, propped up on one elbow. The other is to Alice Bray's second husband, Elizeus Hele, who died in 1636. Carved in alabaster, it depicts not only the recumbent figure of Elizeus in his legal robes, but also the kneeling effigies of his two wives and his twelve-year old son, Walter, by his first wife. The seventeenth-century vicar James Forbes was a vigorous supporter of the monarchy during the Commonwealth. He managed to save the lectern, and at the Restoration triumphantly erected the large carved arms of Charles II, with two accompanying boards lamenting the martyrdom of Archbishop Laud by "that bloody parlement" and the imprisonment of the Bishop of Exeter by that same "wicked parlement". His wife, who died during Cromwell's time, had to be buried outside the church in an odd shrine of 1655.

Facing page above: The cornice.
Facing page below: Pulpit and screen.

BRANSCOMBE
St Winifred

5m/8km E of Sidmouth

In 1909 W. H. Hudson wrote an account of his visits to southern England, published as *Afoot in England*. He describes how he walked from Sidmouth to Branscombe and on the way met a woman who had been born and lived in the village. "There was no sweeter place on earth," she told him. On a paradisaical summer's day, my own path followed his and with a no less beguiling result. Some faint air of Eden hung about this combe. All around flourished the blue and green of a good summer's morning. The fields were bright with wild flowers and young crops of grass from where I viewed the monumental tower of Branscombe's famous church.

Its rare dedication to St Winifred (a little-known seventh-century north Welsh saint) suggested to Hoskins that "a church existed here almost since that time". Whatever the origins of the building, it is clear that the massive central tower and part of the nave are late Norman; the transepts and western half of the nave are thirteenth-century; and the chancel early fourteenth. The exceptionally beautiful clear-glass five-light East window (through which a pink-flowering horse chestnut could be seen swaying in the breeze) was installed by Bishop Neville of Exeter in the mid-fifteenth century.

The interior is rewarding, not only on account of the harmonious serenity of its architecture but for its fine oak furnishings: there is a rare eighteenth-century three-decker pulpit, one of only two in Devon, like a great piece of sculpture in the spacious transept. There is a seventeenth-century screen, altar rails with twisted barley-sugar balusters, a late sixteenth-century gallery, and some box pews.

I sat in the church for some time with that sense of homecoming which can often be felt when a building is at ease with itself. This, I knew, was a place of order, of remembrance, of vision. A place of silence, too, for not even the sound of a ticking clock could interrupt the overwhelming stillness of the nave. To understand the gravity and mystery of St Winifred's, you are advised to appreciate its presence gradually.

Above 17th-century altar-rails.
Facing page: The three-decker pulpit.

BUCKLAND
IN THE MOOR

St Peter

3m/4km NW of Ashburton

This is an unexpectedly enchanting little church in a marvellous moorland setting, hilltop to hilltop dancing along the horizon. The building lies comfortably in the slope of the ground on its hillside, where it overlooks the wooded slopes of Holne Chase and the valley of the river Webbern. It is, as the brief guide states, " 'up and away' from people and traffic, hustle and bustle".

The interior, largely of the fifteenth century, is characterised by an unsophisticated rusticity. Perfectly proportioned and prayerful in feeling, its greatest treasure is its shapely Norman font, vigorously carved with palmette, rosette, and cable ornament. But it is the whole interior which gives pleasure. Why? Is it the splendid rood-screen with its figures painted on the back and front of the wainscot (see pages 16 & 225)? Is it the fine wagon roof? The light? Or the bowl of flowers, lilac and magenta, whose delicate scent permeated the interior? I don't know. I simply loved the stillness of this place. All those heavy of heart should visit it without delay.

The guide concludes: "The people of this parish thank you for visiting their church and hope that your continued journey holds the peace and tranquillity which you have renewed here. Think of us, and our efforts to maintain this ancient and hallowed place of worship." I do.

Facing page: The Norman font.

CLYST ST LAWRENCE

St Lawrence

5m/8km S of Cullompton

The church of this little community – its population barely reaching a hundred – is an undiscovered delight: another unspoilt simple building.

It dates from the fifteenth century, presumably replacing an earlier building (the list of rectors dates back to Robert de Hille, 1281). It has a tunnel-vaulted nave, cream-coloured walls, several clear-glass windows (with brightly coloured panes – tangerine, red, ultramarine – at the top of their Perpendicular tracery), a dumpy granite Norman font with an ogee-shaped cover, and an Arms of Charles II. One oil lamp, one chandelier (electricity was installed as late as 1957), one harmonium and a massive early eighteenth-century Bible

resting on a no less substantial wooden lectern, complete the inventory of this bewitchingly lovely place – English to the root.

The screen, with its brightly coloured, almost fairground mood, is the interior's most conspicuous feature. Although the tracery is missing, its painted fan vaulting is a delight.

Outside there is a disproportionately tall tower with a figure of the Virgin in a niche halfway up. Note the mediaeval cross in the churchyard and the rectory across the lane.

If, in our modern cities, we are in danger of losing the poetry of existence, here at Clyst St Lawrence we find it to the full.

COLDRIDGE
St Matthew

4m/6km E of Winkleigh

You climb the steepish hill, cross the cobbled path to the church, and enter. But first make sure to stop and admire in the churchyard the six dark massive Irish yews, the sturdy tower and the porch's patterned floor of cobbled stones.

The medium-sized interior is superb: deeply rural, unaffected and filled with secrets.

Wood is everywhere, chiefly the fine fifteenth-century screen which stretches wall to wall across the nave, a beautiful un-restored brown. There is also a dark umber barrel-vaulted roof; some late mediaeval benches, and the unexpected originality of the carved pulpit, a delicate milky caramel or fawn, its exquisite early fifteenth-century carving of fabulous intricacy. There is also a beautiful parclose screen which divides the chancel from the so-called Evans chapel with its recumbent effigy of Sir John Evans, a keeper of the Marquess of Dorset's deer park at Coldridge and the church's benefactor. But stone contributes its own graver qualities to this wonderful interior: there is a fine granite arcade, a handsome twelfth-century square and columned font, and the loveliest tracery in the clear-glass windows.

COLYTON
St Andrew

3m/4km N of Seaton

Colyton, near where I once lived, is a largely unspoilt small town, amongst the most charming in Devon. It has streets of eighteenth- and nineteenth-century houses grouped around the large late mediaeval church. Its silver grey exterior is handsome, its crossing crowned with a late fifteenth-century octagonal lantern which can be seen all over the town. Without it Colyton would seem diminished, with neither a geographical nor a spiritual centre.

The fifteenth-century interior is light, wide and spacious but largely divided into two, the nave separated from the chancel by the crossing piers which uphold the tower. To the west of the nave there is a composition of three exceptionally large Perpendicular windows, the middle one almost touching the ground and incorporating the west entrance in its design. Their glass is by Hardman (1906).

A special feature of the church is the sumptuous free-standing Renaissance-style monuments in the Pole chapel, and a fifteenth-century one in the chancel. The latter, dating from 1449, is a recumbent figure on a tomb chest with niches, under a row of three crocketed canopies It is for Margaret Beaufort, Countess of Devon, granddaughter of John of Gaunt. The Pole chapel contains memorials to Sir John Pole (d.1658) and Elizabeth, his wife, and to William Pole (d.1587), and his wife. The Poles were the largest landowners in the area. Its stone screen was built by Thomas Brerewood, vicar of Colyton from 1524-44. The other outstanding features are the two brass chandeliers, each holding 36 candles. These were purchased in 1796 for £8.

Elsewhere, in the south transept there is the shaft of a Saxon Cross discovered during repairs after a fire in 1933. It has scrolls with a bird and a lion on the front and interlacing on the sides.

Above: The west windows.
Facing page: Tower and lantern.

CORNWORTHY

St Peter

4m/6km SE of Totnes

From a distance, seen through the arch of the mediaeval gatehouse of the ruined Cornworthy Priory, the church presents a picturesque prospect, appearing like an eighteenth-century topographical watercolour. Closer up, it is even more attractive.

Mainly of mediaeval construction (*c*.1350-75), it has walls and a battlemented tower built of a local slatey rock, enhanced with beautiful grey lichens. Nave and aisles are separated by five granite piers and arcades of Gothic but almost round-headed arches. There are windows of clear glass and the plaster walls are painted white, giving the interior the impression of a virginal purity. It is, as the guidebook says, "light, bright, simple and largely unspoiled". It is also intelligently and exquisitely cared for.

A licence in the Exeter Faculty Books goes a long way to explaining its Georgian elegance: it was entirely refitted in 1788. There is a magisterial pulpit (1757) with a large sounding board topped by a trumpeting angel, and many early nineteenth-century box pews with handsome, sturdy cone-shaped pinnacles at their back corners. There are panelling and window seats, an exquisite eighteenth-century brass candelabrum, and from an earlier period a barrel vault, a fifteenth-century rood-screen and, in the chancel, a quietly charming Jacobean monument. This is of Sir Thomas Harris and his wife, both recumbent under a low tester decorated with strap work, all lightly coloured but powdery.

The small mediaeval Lady Chapel was restored in 1968, and contains an altar of a block of granite from the ruined Priory of Augustinian Canonesses. On its east wall hangs a carving of an angel's wing which its creator, the sculptor, Jilly Sutton, carved out of a piece of ash wood found on Dartmoor (1997). Having suffered the visual discomfort of countless contemporary altar cloths, red fitted carpets, inappropriately designed tapestried hassocks and modishly 'contemporary' nave lights, I found it a pleasure to encounter the lyrical reticence of this subtle work.

Above: The wife of Sir Thomas Harris, 1610.

CREDITON
The Holy Cross

8m/12km NW of Exeter

Every time I pass the parish church of Crediton, I am reinspired by the compelling nobility of this wonderful building. The long narrow High Street suddenly opens out, and there it sits, in a space all its own, surrounded by tall trees. With its Indian-red castellated walls of sandstone, clear glass clerestory windows and noble tower reminiscent of Exeter Cathedral, its exterior is a magnificent achievement – one of Devon's finest town churches.

The lower part of the tower, crossing, Lady Chapel and southern vestry of the present building survive from the Norman period, but most of the church, comprehensively rebuilt in the fifteenth century, is in the Perpendicular style. From 1848 until 1877 and again in 1913 it was extensively restored.

The best of its contents are the finely carved decorated Easter Sepulchre (with much pinky mediaeval colour remaining), a Norman font, and a three-seater sedilia. Otherwise the interior strikes me as muddled, cluttered and dull. Much of it – the choir stalls, nave benches and most of the glass – is uninspiring. The memorial to General Sir Redvers Buller (by W. D. Caröe) is

overbearing, the wooden sculpture of St Boniface by Witold Kawalec undistinguished. However, the late fourteenth-century monument to a recumbent Sir John Scully and his wife presents an entirely different level of achievement.

Crediton was the birthplace c.680 of St Boniface, who took Christianity to central Germany. In 739 a minster was established in the town, and the first diocesan church was built in 909. This served as the cathedral when a see was established, with a succession of nine bishops, culminating in the eleventh century with Leofric, who obtained permission from the Pope to remove the see to Exeter. A new church, the one we largely see today, was subsequently made collegiate, until it was bought by the parishioners at the Dissolution.

Above: The Easter Sepulchre.
Facing page: The west end, showing clerestory windows.

CULLOMPTON

St Andrew

5m/8km SE of Tiverton

It is a great experience to approach this church, as resplendent as any in Devon. It has a noble, Somerset-style sandstone tower, richly embossed with decorations in whitish Beer stone and crowned with proud battlements and crocketed pinnacles. It is a hundred feet high, and was built between 1545-9. I have a feeling that from the encircling hills, this tower, like a Madonna della Misericordia, would be seen to protect and dominate the town.

On entering you are struck by an interior of Handelian splendour and assurance. Wool paid for this church, whose creation coincided with Cullompton's most prosperous years. There is a grand, six-bay nave dating from *c*.1450, aisles of *c*.1500, and on the south side of the church the spectacular Lane aisle of *c*.1526. This is famously distinguished by its exotic fan vaulting, like something out of The Arabian Nights, and by its display of emblems which refer to my namesake's sources of wealth as a wool trader (see page 208). The aisle is generously lit from a series of large windows, which no longer provide the mystical light of the early Middle Ages but the confident illumination of the dawning age of Humanism.

A superb panelled and wagon roof runs the whole length of the building. It is richly worked and painted, with much of its original gilding and colouring intact. No less glorious is the marvellous screen which extends across the entire width of the church, its five bands of embellished carving dimly glowing with sombre gilt, its pillars painted with coloured stripes like an old-fashioned barber's pole.

In the south aisle, a unique survival: the Golgotha, a skull and crossbones. It is black and massive, the original base of the church's rood-beam which held the Crucifix, rigorously carved with rocks, skulls and bones.

Above: Fan vaulting in the Lane aisle.
Facing page: The wagon roof runs right through the nave and chancel.

DARTMOUTH

St Saviour

7m/11km SE of Totnes

Tucked away at the bottom of a hill amongst the crowded back lanes of the old port, St Saviour's hides its rich picturesque interior behind severe grey walls. Yet on entering all is revealed: the highly painted and gilded screen, the two brass chandeliers and the vividly coloured late fifteenth-century pulpit are a song to friendliness and comfort. Few interiors can match this degree of exuberance.

Its dominant feature is the spectacular screen with its perfect coving and splendidly carved friezes in the cornice. Accounts exist for its construction in 1496. The colour and carving of this beautiful object are as luxuriant as a fruiting apple tree after a good summer. No less gorgeous is the adjacent stone pulpit (1490). Here again, ripeness is all.

As you enter the church, you cannot miss the mediaeval metalwork on the south porch door; two virile leopards (with their rear legs forming the hinges) stretching across the leafy branches of a tree of life. The energy of this design, its confident male power, is astounding. Carbon testing has shown the age of the door's woodwork could be prior to 1372, the date of the church's consecration. The date of 1631 on the door itself presumably refers to a restoration.

The parclose screens and the communion table are Elizabethan, as are the painted wooden figures of the Evangelists on the altar. The magnificent west gallery, with carvings commemorating the Armada, was erected in 1633. There is a prominent piscina and sedilia.

Throughout the fourteenth century, thriving on the wine trade with France, Dartmouth enjoyed considerable prosperity – after Exeter, Plymouth and Barnstaple, it was the fourth town in Devon. Of all the merchants and shipmasters of the mediaeval port, John Hawley, several times Mayor of Dartmouth, was the greatest. He gave most of the money for the building of the church and is shown as a knight with his two wives on the largest and finest brass in Devon (under the chancel carpet). It is probable that Chaucer, who visited the town in his role as Inspector of Customs, met Hawley in 1373, and maybe based his Shipman upon him.

Above: Leopard on door.
Facing page: Pulpit and screen.

EXETER
St David

St David's Hill

Built in 1897-1900 to the designs of William Douglas Caröe, and probably his finest church, St David's is a very handsome building. The exterior built of grey limestone, roughly tooled with dressings of Bath and Portland stone, is an important landmark on St David's Hill. It has a particularly distinctive design, busy, idiosyncratic and robust.

The architecture of the Bath stone interior has a warm, quiet dignity. The generous volume of the nave, with its dark timber tunnel-vault (originally stained green), is bound together by great transverse arches. The tall, narrow aisles, hardly more than passages, are set against the north and south external walls. Craftsmanship is the key to Caröe's treatment of the sedilia and the font tester, the doors with their wrought-iron handles, the copper-winged angels which look down from the roof, and the altar frontal with its delicately painted angels.

In keeping with Caröe's own highly personal version of a free Arts and Crafts Gothic, the building is characterised by a number of prominent features. These include the quality of its craftsmanship, the employment of local materials and the rejection of any crude mass-produced fittings.

Above: Sedilia.
Facing page: Details from lectern, pulpit and font.

BAPTISM

EXETER

St Martin

Cathedral Close

At one time there were about fifteen mediaeval churches within the city walls. Of these only seven remain with fabric older than the nineteenth century: St Mary Arches, St Mary Steps, St Olave, St Pancras, St Petrock, St Stephen and St Martin, which I am including here because of its proximity to the cathedral and indisputable beauty. According to Jean Gimpel in *The Cathedral Builders*, in the Middle Ages there was a church or chapel for every 200 inhabitants or thereabouts. But today, since so few actually live in the centre of the city, the old centres of worship have become largely redundant. Since 1995 St Martin's has been cared for by the Churches Conservation Trust.

The first building on this site was consecrated on 6 July 1065 by Bishop Leofric, who founded the Cathedral. Early in the fifteenth century, St Martin's was enlarged and remodelled, and in the eighteenth century completely refurnished. It stands modestly in a corner of Cathedral Close.

Basically composed of a nave, chancel and tower painted creamy-pink, all squeezed into a cramped and irregular site (which internally forms its tiny north transept), St Martin's presents another living record of the past. There is mediaeval glass, there are box pews, a pulpit and west gallery of *c.*1700, a reredos of *c.*1710, late seventeenth-century communion rails, and several seventeenth- and eighteenth-century wall monuments, including one to Philip Hooper. This

gentleman, depicted at prayer with a skull and a pile of books, is seen wearing an oversize wig and, in the words of Beatrix Cresswell, "has a complacent smile as if he were occupied neither with books, nor prayers, but was reflecting with satisfaction upon his improvements in the church". Besides its tower, the church has a big west window of Beer stone facing the Cathedral, prominent and beautiful.

St Martin's escaped the Victorian restoration and the bombing which damaged both the Cathedral and St Stephen's in the High Street. It retains a delightful atmosphere of the Middle Ages and the eighteenth century combined. It has a comely feeling, at once intimate and unselfconscious. Easy to find, always open. Visit it.

Above: The church is tucked away in a corner of Cathedral Close.

HACCOMBE
St Blaise

3m/4km E of Newton Abbot

Situated amongst gleaming, golden fields, this little church was built by St Stephen de Haccombe after his return from the Fifth Crusade. It is towerless but of the thirteenth century and externally very simple. Its interior (difficult of access) consists of a nave and chancel separated from the south aisle by four pointed, unusually thick, red sandstone arches supported by short octagonal columns without plinths. Later additions include the chancel screen, reredos and pulpit designed in 1821 by John Kendall, then architect of Exeter Cathedral. They are of a Gothick character, attractive, and carved in white Beer stone.

However St Blaise is less notable for its architecture than its remarkable collection of mediaeval effigies and brasses of various lords

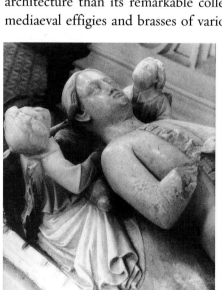

of Haccombe. The earliest are the three sepulchral figures of the later thirteenth century: a cross-legged knight (possibly Sir Stephen de Haccombe), a lady wearing a wimple, and another lady also wearing a wimple and holding a book. There are also two figures, a knight and his lady, recumbent on a large tomb chest and, remarkably, an alabaster effigy of a youth in civilian dress – only two foot two inches long, an enchanting miniature. The angels at his head are particularly beautiful.

The church possesses an exceptional collection of inlaid mediaeval tiles, some made locally and some in Exeter, about 400 in number and of 29 different designs (see page 248).

Above, top: Brass of Sir Nicholas Carew, 1469.
Above, left: Late 14th-century miniature alabaster effigy of a youth, supported by angels.

HARTLAND

St Nectan

4m/6km W of Clovelly

Hartland is a small town and an immense parish, occupying the lonely peninsula in the extreme north-west corner of Devon, which according to W. G. Hoskins, "contains the most impressive cliff scenery in England and Wales".

Inland, the landscape is Cornish – wind-swept, buzzard-haunted and remote in feeling – as is the church of St Nectan, which can be seen from a considerable distance against the Atlantic. It is about two miles from Hartland, its giant, gaunt, dark-grey fifteenth-century tower rising above a huddle of farms and bungalows at the hamlet of Stoke. The highest in north Devon at 130 feet, it served as a beacon to mariners on this treacherous coast. The dedication is to St Nectan, a Celtic saint whose mediaeval statue survives on the tower's east face.

Within moments of arrival you know that you have come to an enchanted place: the lonely landscape, the sea-washed sky, announce something of its healing power. Opening the porch door onto silence, you enter a remarkable interior. Nothing jars. Nothing is too sumptuous; nothing too rich or dull. But the mood, rinsed in an autumn melancholy, is elevating. I have visited this church for many years and it still preserves the same magic it had for me in the 1960s – its sombre grandeur, its wintry loveliness and otherworldliness.

The interior, paved with beautiful ash-grey slates and lit by clear-glass windows, astonishes because of its extraordinary scale. The style is the Perpendicular of the late fourteenth century, subject to a restoration, particularly of the windows, in 1848. But there is much else to appreciate in this noble building: the limestone piers of the arcades (four in the nave and one in the chancel); the all-through wagon roofs, some painted with large stars; the Norman font (see page 217) and the spectacular wooden screen (*c*.1470). Nearly 48 feet long, it spans the entire building and has a coving and cornice burgeoning with fruits and vegetation. But that is not all. There are bench ends of 1530, numerous mural monuments, a slate slab commemorating the publishers John and Allen Lane of the Hartland Abbey family, and, curiously, a chair upon which the Emperor of Ethiopia, Haile Selassie, sat when he visited the church in 1938. Above the north porch there is a priest's chamber in which the Cornish poet and antiquary, Parson Hawker of Morwenstow, wrote *The Cell by the Sea*.

The pews are notorious for their discomfort; but centuries of words – sermons, readings, marriage vows, funeral orations – have been heard by congregations sitting upon them. Centuries of poetry and centuries of teaching.

HITTISLEIGH
St Andrew

7m/11km SW of Crediton

To reach this hidden place we travelled through miles of steep and winding lanes barely wider than the car. July now and high summer, the upland fields are browning, the hedge grasses yellowing, the moor alive with insects.

Hittisleigh is a wonderful country church, as fresh as a dairy and of a simple beauty. I sit in its cool cream-washed and plastered interior enjoying the stillness, the sounds of birds, and the

sight of the unpretentious features spread before me – the fifteenth-century granite piers, the old flagstone flooring, the Norman font, the brocaded altar frontal, the polished brass lectern, the hanging paraffin lamps, a bowl of flowers and the row of deeply-set lattice windows sparkling in today's sunshine – memorials of centuries of devoted attention.

This moorland church has no pretensions to grandeur, but as its rector writes in an excellent booklet, "It is all the more endearing and special because of its simplicity. It serves as the modest focus for a modest spread of our Parish made up of scattered hamlets and homesteads. We love it and want to share and celebrate our love." I certainly do, and want to thank those who care for this beautiful sanctuary.

HONEYCHURCH
St Mary

7m/11km E of Hatherleigh

Amongst all the parish churches of Devonshire, Honeychurch is probably my favourite. I love its rustic simplicity, its unpretentiousness and convincing earthiness. It speaks to me of the timeless Devon before urbanisation eroded the old rural civilisation and replaced it with a suburban culture of neither town nor country. Of course, Honeychurch lacks the sumptuous richness of the churches of Ottery St Mary or Cullompton; its glory is otherwise, a reminder of the Christ-like humility of the Elizabethan divine, George Herbert.

The building itself lies off a farm lane in remote countryside; its little porch faces Dartmoor. Entering, one is surprised by its smallness and rusticity, its silence. Honeychurch has an unsophisticated interior, almost untouched since the twelfth century: a nave and chancel divided by a simple granite arch. There is a Norman font (see page 215), an Elizabethan pulpit complemented by the Elizabethan arms painted on the north wall, and a collection of rustic pews. On either side of the entrance door are two Norman beast heads. The floor is covered with ancient boards. Except for the light, that's about all there is to find here.

W. G. Hoskins loved this place too. Reflecting upon the spiritual life of the mediaeval centuries, he instances Honeychurch as getting nearer to their heart than anywhere else he knows. "We push open the heavy door, and with it the centuries roll back: this withdrawn Norman church on the site of one even older, small and airless, only a plain nave and chancel: there was never any need to enlarge the church at Honeychurch. There at the back under the curtained tower arch, is the mutilated font of Bishop Bartholomew's time, crowned unevenly by a worn, slightly comic, cover of Jacobean date; here are the wormy benches of rustic carpentry – some 15th-century carpenter from Sampford Courtenay no doubt made them – the pulpit from which the doctrines of the Elizabethan Church were first to be heard, the curtains, the plastered and bossed roof, the plain granite chancel arch. It is all so worn and uneven, not a straight line anywhere, soaked with so many centuries of the Latin Mass spoken to a small gathering of Devonshire farmers and labourers and their households. In the light from the clear glass of the windows, we almost hear again the mumbled Litanies and Collects on 18th-century Sunday mornings, the murmur of the Lord's Prayer and the Psalms spoken in broad Devonshire voices, the immemorial words of the English Sunday they knew by heart."

KENN
St Andrew

5m/8km S of Exeter

The journey from Kenton is an exhilarating one. Leaving the high ridge of Great Haldon to the south-west, travelling under the blackest of skies – the soil red, the road scarlet, the grasses bejewelled with raindrops – we reached Kenn, whose parish lies in the fertile valley of that name.

The building, which lies beyond a monumental yew, is built out of a dark and beautiful red sandstone, mottled with spots of whitish lichen. Its porch, red and crumbly like the crust of home-baked soda bread, invites entry. Opening the heavy church door, I once more experience the familiar feeling of exultation.

In fact the interior is a shock: St Andrew's is a thickly atmospheric place, mysterious, essentially Victorian, but with a homely, even comely feel. There are dark sandstone walls and pillars, and a series of late Victorian and exceptionally attractive stained glass windows of the Life of Christ made by Hardman & Co. The east window has a representation of Christ in Majesty, and the big Perpendicular windows of the aisles show seven scenes from the Life of Christ. The Resurrection with a group of sleeping soldiers in the first window in the south aisle is especially good.

However, it is the screen (*c*.1500) with its painted panels of saints which attracts most attention. The saints on the north side are men, those on the south side, apart from the four Evangelists on the door of the Lady Chapel, are women, including Saint Bridget of Sweden and a rare image of Saint Mary of Egypt, one of only four in this country, carrying her three loaves. Known as the Whore of Egypt, she retreated into the desert for 45 years as an act of penance, and emerged with her loaves intact and her sainthood assured. In the centre panel there is an unusual depiction of a lily crucifix.

The church contains a large number of ancient pews, some fifteenth- or sixteenth-century bench ends, and the oldest object in the church, a Norman font made of Purbeck marble.

Above: Fifteenth-century stained glass in vestry.

KINGS NYMPTON
St James the Apostle

3m/4km N of Chulmleigh

Both internally and externally this is a beautiful church, mainly fifteenth-century, with a massive early-sixteenth west tower and a recently renewed spire. The village name comes from the Celtic word *nemeton*, meaning a sacred place or grove. Thus before the arrival of Christianity in this remote district, Kings Nympton may have been a consecrated place. It remains such today.

Entering this church always provides a shock of delight. Its Georgian fittings (box pews, pulpit and altar rails), its perfect late mediaeval nut-brown screen, its wagon roofs with their carved bosses and the celure above the screen, which Ann Jellicoe has described as "a visual Hallelujah Chorus", are all beautiful. It is worth travelling a considerable distance to discover and enjoy such unassuming loveliness. Inside the tower is a ringing chamber and a long ancient oak ladder. It leads to the loft with its six bells (restored in 1996). The church also has a beautiful cross-ribbed unceiled wagon roof above the south porch. Only the red spotted carpet jars.

The churchyard is special. It is beautifully sited and looks westwards over a green and fertile landscape, wonderful in the unexpectedly bright May light. There are, the guidebook tells us, many graves of families still living in the parish. I especially enjoy the tombstone of the midwife, Mary Lane, who died in 1754:

> *On harmless babes I did attend*
> *While on earth my life did spend.*
> *My hands from pain did many free,*
> *But none from death did rescue me.*
> *My glass is run, my hour is past,*
> *And yours is coming on so fast.*

Above: Screen cornice, cross on painted roof of chancel, and celure.
Facing page: Looking west, into the tower.

MOLLAND

St Mary

6m/10km E of South Molton

One of the lesser-known marvels of Devonshire, Molland church is an almost completely preserved eighteenth-century interior. It contains a complement of 44 box pews (1740s), a canopied three-decker pulpit (with a trumpeting angel on its sounding board), ceiled roofs, slate floors, communion rails, and superb seventeenth- and eighteenth-century monuments, in the main to the Catholic Lords of the Manor, the Courtenays, who at the Reformation took no interest in the preservation of an Anglican church. Clear-glass windows and cream-coloured and plastered walls add to the attraction of this delightful interior.

Further pleasures include the quasi-screen with folding gates, surmounted by a solid plastered

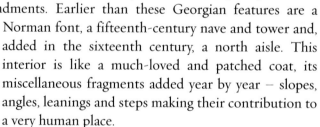

tympanum filling and enclosing the chancel opening. On it (as at Parracombe) are posted the Royal Arms and the Ten Commandments. Earlier than these Georgian features are a

Norman font, a fifteenth-century nave and tower and, added in the sixteenth century, a north aisle. This interior is like a much-loved and patched coat, its miscellaneous fragments added year by year – slopes, angles, leanings and steps making their contribution to a very human place.

The graveyard, overlooking fields, is full of names still found in the village – Cockrams, Pooks, Darts. It is here that the men and women of the parish were buried by the church in which, as children, they had been baptised and married. From Lynton to Plymouth, from Tetcott to Luppitt, the fields of Devon have been tilled, the hedges planted, the ditches dug and the churches built by their forgotten contemporaries.

NEWTON ABBOT

St Luke, Milber

E of town, in Milber

The 1930s was not a decade which saw much distinguished architecture in Devon, but there is at least one exception. It is a church built to serve a housing estate a mile south-east of Newton Abbot: the church of St Luke in Milber. The building was based on a vision by a Devon man, the Rev. J. Keble Martin (author and illustrator of *British Flora*).

It was on 11th March 1931 that Keble Martin experienced an "odd and vivid" dream in which he attended a crowded evening service at a church which did not then exist. The following morning he made a note of its unusual design: no screen dividing clergy from the congregation, but in its place an open sanctuary in immediate contact with the congregation; no Gothic nave but in its place three radiating 'transepts'. His brother Arthur, an architect, interpreted this conception, and a start was made on the building in 1936. The war interrupted, and it was not finally consecrated until 1963.

St Luke's is an undoubted success. There is something of the Byzantine about it, and paradoxically something modern, too. It is indeed dreamlike, and yet, with its Cornish granite columns, earthy. The spacious interior is flooded with natural light and painted a radiant white; its apsidal sanctuary, curved ceiling and harmonious arches add to its ethereal feeling. That a church should be a chamber of light is a post-Reformation notion, but one reinterpreted in a strange new idiom here.

A curiosity of the design is that when Arthur completed the plans he found that its measurements, quite unintentionally, were exactly a thousand inches long, a thousand inches wide and a thousand inches high.

NEWTON ABBOT
St Mary, Wolborough

1m/2km SW of town centre

A pure, bright, sun-rich morning was my introduction to this isolated and rather countrified parish church which stands on a hill commanding views of the Teign estuary and (to the north) the town of Newton Abbot. Melodious birdsong, and a churchyard reputed to be the second largest in England, added their different vernal charms.

The nave is spacious, brightly lit and handsome. There are stately piers and aisles of six bays, their capitals unusually varied and fresh for a building of the fifteenth to early sixteenth century, with bold leaves, an owl and a pig amongst their designs. It has an attractive early-twentieth-century oak barrel roof and some fine nineteenth-century stained-glass windows, of which the three by the Kempe studios are outstanding (especially the one of Evangelists in the middle of the north wall). There is also a window of bits and pieces of mediaeval glass at the western end of the south aisle

The general colour of the nave is cool and white, which provides an attractive foil for the vermilion and gold of the rood-screen. This stretches across both nave and aisles, with parclose screens to the transeptal chapels. The whole is richly coloured, with 66 figures probably painted by the monks of Torre in the early sixteenth century. The brass eagle lectern is late fifteenth century. The red sandstone font with its cable and chevron moulding is Norman.

On the north wall of the chancel is a large memorial to Sir Richard and Lady Lucie Reynell dated 1634, both recumbent and resting on a marble slab supported on coupled Ionic columns. Beneath them and propped up on her elbow lies Sir Richard's daughter, and on the ground, a charming swaddled infant. On the bare white wall behind the monument there are two standing figures of Justice and Time holding an hour-glass. Time looks a trifle resigned to the boredom of his eternal fate.

Above: Aisle capital with floral design.
Facing page: Stained glass angel by Kempe in north aisle.

NORTHLEW
St Thomas of Canterbury

6m/10km NW of Okehampton

From Highhampton I approached the village of Northlew through several miles of springtime – folded valleys, burgeoning hedgerows, clouds of cow parsley and the spume of the flowering wild cherry – on what was, I felt sure, the most beautiful day the world had ever seen. The dark, mole-coloured church lies off the open square around which the village has been built. It has an attractive churchyard crowded with tombstones, a row of large Irish yews and a lime and sycamore in delicate leaf.

The effect of the interior has an exultant quality: there is dark wood, there are granite columns, carved bench ends of 1537 (see page 207), a wagon roof in the north aisle with angels and exuberant flower-shaped bosses (see page 228). Across the width of the nave is a handsome screen and rood-loft; also a powerful Norman font with carved saltire crosses and rosettes on which was standing an exquisite vase of violet primulas.

Although the church reveals evidence of twelfth-century work, including the lower portion of the tower, most of it dates from the fifteenth century. In 1884 it was restored by R. M. Fulford, but Harry Hems was responsible for the new pulpit, lectern and altar. A Table of Continuity on the west wall indicates that the first rector was Richard de Boleville (instituted on May 20th 1258), and that he was succeeded by one Henry, whose surname is not recorded. Since Henry's time there have been 60 rectors including the present one, the Rev. Stuart Wilson.

A memorial in the churchyard records the War dead. In the First World War, the village lost more than a third of its population.

I sat in the nave for some time; it was still and silent, with only the ticking clock and the crick, crick of busy rooks.

Above: Bosses in north aisle chapel.
Facing page: Norman font and Easter flowers.

OTTERY ST MARY
St Mary the Virgin

11m/18km E of Exeter

Ottery St Mary is one of the three or four most beautiful towns in Devon, and the church lives up to its position on a hill in the green valley of the River Otter. With its twin towers over the transepts, it lies squat and leonine in a churchyard surrounded (at least on its eastern side) by attractive colour-washed eighteenth-century houses. There are high gables and austere groups of lancets.

The interior is long and highly decorated. The view from the nave extends through the crossing into the chancel. The two prominent features of this stretch are the vaults – comparable, says Pevsner, with those at Wells and Bristol. The design of the chancel vault with its figured bosses is wonderful. One boss represents Bishop Grandison (see left), who instigated the rebuilding in 1342, using the new cathedral at Exeter as a model. The vaulting of the nave with its magnificent figured bosses, probably created by the carvers of those in the nave of Exeter Cathedral, is also superb. Both nave and aisle roofs are bright with white, red and blue paint.

The prominent effigies are a special delight of this large creamy-coloured interior: they rest beneath fine ogee-headed canopies with thick crocketing and large filials on either side in the second bay of the nave. These are of Bishop Grandison's brother, Sir Otho (d.1359) and his wife Beatrix (d.1374). Also special is the back of the altar screen, the richly canopied stone sedilia, the fourteenth-century choir stalls and the minstrels' gallery. No less delightful is the fan vaulting of the Dorset Aisle. In this part of the building, look out for the capitals formed of scrolls, vine leaves and corbel heads portraying a Green Man, an owl and the head of an elephant. The stained glass in the east and clerestory windows is by John Hardman to designs by Pugin. Bishop Grandison's vitally alive gilded eagle lectern, to be found in the Lady Chapel, is the oldest in England. The polychromatic marble font by William Butterfield is a magnificent achievement (see page 214). Butterfield was also responsible for the wall decoration in the south transept.

Although it is often considered one of the finest of Devon's churches, in my judgement it is in places rather a visual muddle.

Above: Boss of Bishop Grandison.
Facing page: Chancel vaulting.

PARRACOMBE
St Petrock

4m/6km SW of Lynton

This is a building and a site worth travelling many miles to experience. It is as natural an element in the landscape as the country which lies close to hand, and has an interior unaltered for 200 years. The exterior, long and low, with its twelfth- or thirteenth-century massive bastion of a tower, fits snugly into its hillside setting. There are views of the moors from the churchyard.

St Petrock was a Cornish saint who is believed to have died at Bodmin on 4th July 564. There are four churches in Cornwall and eight in Devon bearing his name; the one at Parracombe may well have stood here from soon after his day. Today the building consists of a nave, chancel, south aisle, south porch, north-west tower and north vestry. The tower was built in 1182 and the chancel in 1252, but their survival was something of a close thing

Back in 1879 fears were expressed for the stability of St Petrock's, and it was proposed that it should be demolished and a new church built on the site. The suggestion incurred a wave of protest, and the great art and social critic John Ruskin headed the list of those who declared that it should be preserved because it was so beautiful. St Petrock's was saved and a new building, Christ Church, was built in the centre of the village lower down the hill. In 1969, the original church was made redundant, and since 1971 has been cared for by the Churches Conservation Trust – the first in the whole of England to be recommended for preservation by the Advisory Board for Redundant Churches, as the Conservation Trust was originally called. Today there are only about 70 churches which still preserve intact the 'Prayer-Book' interiors once familiar to all who worshipped in an Anglican church between around 1570 and the 1840s.

For the indisputable charm of St Petrock's lies in its completely unspoiled Georgian interior. There is an eighteenth-century screen with a solid tympanum above it (upon which have been painted the Royal Arms, Commandments, Creed, and Lord's Prayer), a pulpit with a sounding board, a minister's reading desk with a clerk's seat attached, and a large number of eighteenth-century high box pews which rise theatrically at the back, where the musicians sat. St Petrock's was supposedly the last church in Devon in which the singing was supported by a band of musicians.

PLYMOUTH
Church of the Ascension

Crown Hill Estate

The colours of this large, calm, luminous interior are relatively easy to describe. It has a burgundy roof, an east end composed of dark grey natural stone, punctuated by a group of small hexagonal windows filled with strongly-coloured glass which gleam in the morning sun. There is a cream-coloured baldacchino and pews. The columns, pencil-thin, are a light grey. But it is more difficult to describe the architecture, at once inventive and self-conscious, attractive and stately in a 1950s idiom, which here prefigures Basil Spence's design for Coventry Cathedral. Before my visit, I had seen photographs of both the interior and exterior, and had wondered whether the church was worth visiting. Having been there I can say definitely: yes, it is. The interior is unpretentious and worshipful. I liked its huge unobstructed clear-glass windows and its overall sense of uncluttered space, its consoling spirit of peace. I also liked the way it was placed like other post-war churches as the focus of a spacious upland housing estate.

The year 1956 was not an auspicious one for designing churches in this country, but in the late 1940s and early 1950s Matisse had created the Chapel of the Rosary at Vence, and between 1950 and 1953 Le Corbusier had designed another masterpiece at Ronchamp. The architect of this church, Robert Potter, was inspired by Sir Ninian Comper rather than these European masters, but his work at Crown Hill is a fresh achievement. He created a church in a modern idiom in which a modern congregation could feel comfortably at home.

Above: West windows, font and internal garden.

PLYMTREE

St John the Baptist

3m/4km SE of Cullompton

This is the perfect country church and, as Pevsner claims, one of the most attractive in Devon. In all that fresh and spacious interior each feature contributes towards its perfection. Nothing could be added to improve the whole.

The walls are plastered and whitewashed, the lighting luminously clear, the proportions elegant, the mood serene – its interior has something of the exultant purity of a Byrd motet, and something of its solace, too.

It is rich with unpretentious treasures: old pews and bench ends; seventeenth-century panelling and altar-rails; a plain eighteenth-century pulpit; and, unexpectedly, a Flemish alabaster relief of the Resurrection (*c.*1600) on the west wall.

But it is the rood-screen which is the chief glory of the church. In form it is the usual fan-vaulted type, but with its golden sheen, exquisite carving, fourfold cornice and on its lower panels a complete set of 36 painted figures, it is as fine as any in Devon. Some of the paintings are biblical, some local: here is St Sidwell with the scythe that cut off her head, and here St Arimathea with the two cruets which supposedly contained Christ's blood and sweat.

Note, too, the textures and colours of the interior – the cream-coloured columns, the white plaster walls, the gilded woodwork, the dark umber benches and grey flagstones. The building was sensitively restored by William Weir who later undertook the restoration of Dartington Hall.

On the Perpendicular tower there is a mediaeval statue of the Virgin, and in the graveyard a great yew, supposedly 1,100 years old. In all probability it replaced a ritual tree of the Saxons, perhaps even the Celts, and the village was named after it. In the Middle Ages, Plymtree was a stopping point for pilgrims travelling to Glastonbury from the Devon ports.

Above: Detail of Flemish alabaster of the Resurrection.
Facing page: South aisle looking west.

SAMPFORD COURTENAY

St Andrew

5m/8km NE of Okehampton

The approach is an inspiration. The road travels through deep, rarely visited countryside, up and down little folded hills, curving left and right until the pinnacles of the church tower are seen sticking up like the pricked-up ears of an expectant hare.

This tower, built of ashlar, is a proud and mighty presence; the south side of the church, like an elaborate Gothic reliquary, is no less distinguished. The porch is approached down a sloping path leading through a graveyard whose ancient trees are inhabited by rooks. The churchyard is often noisy with their cawing and croaking; sometimes, too, with the clangour of pealing bells.

Through an ancient, oatmeal-coloured door (see page 213), the interior is spacious, light-filled, exceptionally large and comfortable in spirit; it has an aristocratic feeling imbued with a peaceful lyricism. The nave is of an exceptional width. The south arcade is of two dates and two different stones: the four westernmost bays are of polyphant, a beautiful dove-grey stone from Cornwall, and the two bays beyond the screen of early sixteenth-century granite, There are good wagon roofs and some exceptional bosses. One, of great distinction, is of a Green Man, but there is also a wheel of three rabbits and a sow with her piglets.

The church is flooded with light from its many clear-glazed windows. Other attractive features include a fine Norman font (see page 214), a plain eighteenth-century pulpit, and a short section of screen to the south chapel, reconstructed in 1923 by Herbert Read.

The village is filled with whitewashed cob and thatched cottages, a peaceful scene. But it was not always so. It was in Sampford Courtenay that the doomed Prayer Book Rebellion of 1549 had its Devonian origins. Its consequences were bloody (it left at least 3,000 men dead and the West Country traumatised), but today's village, at peace with itself, gives no indication of that historic turmoil.

Above: Boss of Green Man in the chancel roof.

SATTERLEIGH
St Peter

4m/6km SW of South Molton

This charming little church is situated in an enchanting place. It is close to the heart of a working farmyard in the hills above the valley of the river Mole. A tiny, aisleless, poetic place, it is difficult to find, but not to be missed on any account.

Essentially a fifteenth-century building, St Peter's consists of a nave, a south porch and, on its western gable, a weatherboarded bell-cote. The mediaeval door is probably original. There is a fifteenth-century font and a richly carved celure of somewhat later date over the site of the rood, west of the original screen. This no longer exists, but the tympanum over it remains, painted in late Georgian times with The Lord's Prayer and The Creed. The Ten Commandments are on large boards on either side of the east window.

Although the church was much restored in 1852, when the chancel was rebuilt, the feeling inside is of an arrangement for seventeenth- or eighteenth-century worship, with its pulpit, sounding board and reading desk, a solid tympanum and several homely runs of hat pegs. The Royal Arms over the door are dated 1726. All is seemly, as George Herbert requested.

In 1801 the population of Satterleigh was 64, much the same as it had been in 1642, but by the 1901 census it had suffered a grievous fall – to 55. The present population is about 40. The church is in the care of the Churches Conservation Trust.

Facing page: Looking from the porch into the church.

SHALDON

St Peter

Outskirts of Teignmouth on S side of River

This is a remarkable building, a reinvention of the Gothic spirit and a superlative example of Arts and Crafts inventiveness. It was constructed between 1893 and 1902, and lies parallel to the river on the far (north) side of the long bridge over the Teign.

The architect was Edmund Sedding, the nephew of the better-known J. D. Sedding, designer of Holy Trinity, Sloane Street, London, who shared his uncle's preference for the inspiration of nature and urge to break away from strict conformity to the Gothic style.

The effect of entering the church is startling. It has a broad and airy nave lit by a great west window, whose powerful tracery reinterprets the theme of the Crown of Thorns. The same motif reappears in the huge stone and iron chancel screen with its stern pattern of thorny briars. Yes, in a sense this is Gothic, but not the Gothic of the Middle Ages. This is Gothic of a new kind. Sedding's belief that the artist could "entice the soul of the tangled thicket into the mazes of his carved and beaten work" is given literal expression here.

St Peter's is a big building, sombre in mood but enlivened by fascinating invention. The use of colour is particularly wonderful – look, for instance, at the pulpit (*c*.1910) with its base of black marble, supports of eight salmon-coloured round columns and a pedestal of blue-grey marble tinged with pink, the whole surmounted by a curved rim of dark chocolate stone gleaming like a pair of polished shoes.

There is a barrel-vaulted nave upheld by tall eight-sided piers of polyphant stone with narrow arcades and a chancel, a Lady Chapel, an apse, and many further astonishing details. Note in particular the carved angels on the marble frontal and the five large statuary figures – Saints Peter, John, Nicholas, Paul and the Virgin Mary – on the rood-screen. The calm figure of St John the Baptist (carved by Henry Wilson), who bears a clamshell containing the water of the font, is an especially imaginative touch.

The spirit of the apsidal Sanctuary is devotional; the lighting is mysteriously dim, and the six candlesticks are most sensitively illuminated.

Above: Angel on the communion rail.
Facing page: Devon marble pulpit and stone screen.

SIDBURY
St Giles & St Peter

3m/4km N of Sidmouth

The winding lane from East Budleigh to Sidbury passes through a landscape verdant and wooded, with gleams of sea, ox-blood cliffs, fertile hills and in the town of Sidmouth delightful Regency pink-painted *cottages ornés*. With its well-kept houses, some thatched, others slated, and its grander buildings, Sidbury is a handsome town. In the hot sunshine, the churchyard with its long, uncut grass starred with flowering white daisies provided the setting for this most beautiful church.

This building is of considerable interest. It has mediaeval work of every period, a Norman tower with two twelfth-century carvings in niches on its west wall, a Norman chancel, and a puzzling crypt of uncertain date, possibly of Saxon origin. The walls of the nave with its rounded, buff-coloured Norman piers and aisles were heightened in the middle of the

fifteenth century, when an enormous rebuilding of the church was begun. It was then that the two aisles and their lovely wagon roofs, large and clear-glassed windows and decorated Gothic arches at their eastern ends, were rebuilt. According to Barbara Softly in her excellent guidebook, *Sidbury's Church of a Thousand Years*, the decorated arches which joined the aisles to the transepts are probably of Flemish work, imported in segments from abroad. In the nineteenth century the tower was rebuilt to the original design; the spire added in 1895.

Other treasures include a western gallery (1749) with original colouring – soft blue and gold and simulated marble – surmounted by a trumpeting angel, very grand. There are chancel fittings by Walter Cave of the Sidbury Manor House family, a fifteenth-century font with a charming eighteenth-century cover, stained-glass windows of some quality, and on the east wall of the exterior a puzzling design of squares, cut with an axe and thought to be Norman.

A report of 1301 lists the furniture – "one good chalice, four sets of corporals, three sets of vestments, twenty altar cloths . . . three surplices for boys, a nuptial veil, an ivory pyx bound with silver, candlesticks of fine brass, processional crosses of metal and banners . . . " – all of which, writes Barbara Softly, gives the impression that the church was well looked after and not short of money. I would judge that situation remains unchanged.

Above: Design on east wall.
Facing page: West gallery with trumpeting angel.

STOWFORD
St John

7m/11km E of Launceston

Its granite exterior encrusted with spots of white lichen, St John's is positioned on a gentle hillside and set amongst tall trees. No village as such is to be seen, but a sprawl of houses. The building has an impressive tower, patterned with bands of red sandstone and granite, and with big square pinnacles. Its porch faces a sloping field, and on the day of my visit an apple tree in tight small pink bud was breaking into blossom in the strong spring sunlight.

Entering the building I was faced by a delightful interior: an unexpected but complete mediaeval church. The architect was Sir Gilbert Scott, whose fairly substantial 'restoration' included the addition of the present north aisle, the replacement of the roof, the organ case, the lectern, the font cover, the altar-rails and eight stained-glass windows by Lavers and Barrault. The woodwork, a complete set of 1874 fittings by Harry Hems of Exeter, was based on 300 casts of mediaeval Devon woodwork. If the quality of some of it lacks sensitivity, it is generally pleasing; the stained glass is also attractive. The date for this work is 1872-75; the cost £4,300 or about £4 million in today's money. The wagon roofs of the south aisle, the south chapel and the porch are mediaeval. The chancel is enriched with a series of angels protruding from its corbels; the roof of the nave flickers with touches of gilding.

The church also houses a disproportionately large monument to Christopher Harris, Master to the Household to King George II and III, and his wife, erected according to her will of 1726. He, dressed as a Roman foot soldier, is wearing a fashionable full-bottom wig. It is situated at the west end of the north aisle but is impossible to miss. Rather less ostentatious are the helm and gauntlet at the east end of the south aisle, and the font of possibly Norman origin.

Above top: Monument to John Harris and his wife, 1726.
Above, left: Norman font.

SUTCOMBE

St Andrew

5m/8km N of Holsworthy

Sutcombe is a remote church and parish close to the deserted Cornish border. I travelled there on 25th April 2006, the hottest day of the year so far. In the course of that visit I saw the hedgerow beech trees losing their bronze bud scales and developing a magical green sheen. The primroses were flowering and the wild plum flung its spray like sea spume.

St Andrews is like a poem by Thomas Hardy; wintry but refulgent with the beauty of its natural materials: granite, oak, clear glass, whitewashed stone. It was founded in Norman times, but extended and rebuilt in the fifteenth century, when a chapel was added, the Thuborough aisle. The interior of the church is light and spacious with Perpendicular north and south arcades of five and three bays. There are many bench ends (their tops shiny with fingering); many coloured and decorated mediaeval floor tiles (also worn by the movement of countless feet); ribs and bosses on the wagon roofs; a sixteenth-century carved wooden pulpit; a granite font; a little mediaeval glass; a splendid carved wood screen of individual design; and a number of square-headed Tudor windows flooding the church with spring sunlight.

But the appeal of this place rests not solely in its ancient contents; I was thrilled to see how tenderly it was loved and cared for by the rector and his parishioners. The altar frontal, dressed with a white cloth, a brass cross, two brass candlesticks and vases freshly filled with daffodils, was in itself a work of art. Then a single daffodil lying on the cloth caught my attention; to it was attached a sad memorial which read: "Nutmeg, my little cat and best friend who died yesterday."

The silence, no, not silence . . . the stillness, the poetry of this exquisite place are worth travelling miles to experience. Close to the church are six seventeenth-century stone almshouses with casement windows.

Facing page: Detail of early Renaissance pulpit.

SWIMBRIDGE
St James the Apostle

5m/8km SE of Barnstaple

Park the car near a field of allotments, cross a little humped-back bridge over a rushing stream, and walk through the spacious graveyard to the church with its tower and lead-covered broach spire, which remain from the fourteenth century. The scene is reminiscent of Samuel Palmer's *The Magic Apple Tree*. Indeed, the atmosphere is very pastoral.

Pastoral, too, are the memories of the famous hunting parson John Russell, who was rector here for 48 years from 1833; he bred the Jack Russell Terrier, and is buried in the churchyard.

His church is extremely handsome, even lavish, an opulence due to the Deans of Exeter, with furnishings now polished like treasured heirlooms. The beautifully carved font cover is perhaps the finest in Devon, with folding panels carved with Renaissance motifs, and a richly decorated tester or canopy. But the church's glory is a spectacular screen, 44 feet long and 10 feet high, stretching across the nave and aisles. Its cornice, composed of a tangled mass of knobbly, bossy leaf forms, is as if all of Devon's hedgerows, all her wild flowers, all her banks soft-matted with moss and glowing primroses, her cowslip fields and woods of dog's mercury and wild anemone, had been remembered and celebrated here. These wooden rood-screens, of which about 150 examples remain in Devon, are not only amongst the chief treasures of the churches they adorn, but are surely the county's greatest contribution to art.

The richness of the Swimbridge interior includes its carved stone pulpit (*c*.1490), whose saints retain some of their original colouring, and its marvellous wagon roofs and bench ends,

To the left of the exit on the south wall are two photographs showing the interior before the alterations introduced by J. L. Pearson in 1879-82. There were box pews and a west gallery, giving the church a leaner, plainer appearance. Pearson's restoration was a sensitive one.

To the right of the main door is a monument in memory of John Rosier, Attorney of the Common Bench & an Auntient of the Honourable Society of Lincoln's Inn, who died on 25th December, 1658. The inscription is couched in legal terminology:

> *Loe with a Warrant sealed by God's decree*
> *Death his grim seargeant hath arrested me!*
> *No bayle was to be given: no law could save*
> *My body from the prison of the Grave . . .*

Facing page: Font cover and tester,
with folding panels of Renaissance woodwork.

TAWSTOCK

St Peter

2m/3km S of Barnstaple

The approach to this church must be one of the loveliest in England. It lies on a gently sloping hillside in hidden, timbered parkland, the road edged with daffodils. In front the shining Taw, on the right, the great dome of Codden Hill, and above, the cream-painted Gothick Tawstock Court.

Since the Norman conquest, the lordship of the manor has remained in unbroken succession with the Fitzwarrens, the Bourchiers and the Wreys. On my visit I asked the Rector's wife, Ruth Carvosso, for the word which might best describe the feeling of this place. "Continuity," she replied. "Continuity of prayer, continuity of worship and tradition." Her husband is the 44th Rector in a line stretching back to Philip of Exeter in 1240 and John de Tracey in 1249.

And, as if to prove her point, the church is filled with an extraordinary collection of remarkable monuments, mostly to the Bath family. The earliest is that of Frances, Lady Fitzwarren, who died in 1589, a large six-poster tomb with a recumbent effigy (see page 222). Another grandiloquent memorial is that of William, third Earl of Bath and his wife Elizabeth Russell, dated 1623. That to Henry Bourchier, 5th Earl of Bath, died 1654, is another ostentatious affair: a large black marble sarcophagus at the corners of which are four obelisks, each guarded by a finely carved white dog. The graceful, free-standing, life-size statue of Rachel, Countess of Bath from 1680, and the urn on a large pedestal for Sir Bourchier Wrey from 1784, are no less remarkable. There are others too, no less extravagant, sumptuous, severe; all positioned higgledy-piggledy like wardrobes in a furniture depository. They are the silent annals of England.

The church itself is attractive, its interior moodily poetic. Cruciform in plan, with a central tower, it is almost purely early fourteenth-century in date, an unusual feature in Devon churches. The nave roof is of the unceiled, open-timbered wagon type. Worth looking out for is an eighteenth-century sundial, a ringers' gallery, a collection of carved bench ends, and some exquisitely plastered flowers and tendrils on the ceilings of the transepts.

Facing page: Detail of monument to Henry Bourchier.

TIVERTON

St Peter

12m/19km N of Exeter

One man, the merchant John Greenway, who rose to wealth as a London Merchant Venturer and Draper, was responsible for several of the finest features of this large fifteenth-century town church. It has a Somerset-type western tower and a lofty interior, which are fine, but it is only Greenway's contribution (1517) which is spectacular,

The chapel is a showpiece, its exterior covered with a host of miniature carvings, of which the most attractive is the 'ship frieze' showing with a wealth of detail the type of vessel upon which Greenway had laden his wares. There are traces of Renaissance motifs incorporated in the carvings, and the wooden door to the aisle is also covered with Renaissance pilasters and arabesques. The south porch, also small, has exquisitely carved scenes of the Passion of Christ. and on its roof a lovely stone vault panelled with ogee reticulation and motifs such as eagles

and fish. Finally, above the entrance to the church, there is a very beautiful Assumption of the Virgin flanked by John Greenway and his wife and the initials I. G.

Inside, the creamy-coloured Greenway chapel is unmistakable. It is not accessible from the south aisle but through a small door in the porch. Its shallow vault is richly panelled and decorated with numerous pendants.

In a sense these acts of patronage were an ostentatious display of new wealth. They purchased (or were thought to purchase) both worldly fame and the security of eternal salvation. Yet through them, as John Harvey writes, "God was (also) glorified by means of works seldom equalled and never surpassed by man's hands."

Above: Frieze of ships on Greenway aisle.

TORBRYAN
Holy Trinity

4m/6km SW of Newton Abbot

My first sight was one of amazement, unprepared as I was for the sheer mesmerising presence of a building as unexpected as a unicorn in an English meadow. I saw that this church rose to sublimity. It was superb but extraordinary. From the topmost pinnacles of its tall west tower to the vivid tracery of its Perpendicular windows, it and the adjacent Church House, now an inn, were covered in a white limewash.

Hoskins describes it as "perhaps the most uniformly attractive village church in Devon", and so it is. The interior, approached via a good lychgate and through a porch with a fan-vaulted ceiling, is of great beauty: its white-painted Beer stone arcades, aisles and plastered walls and ceilings make, as Hoskins says, a "perfect foil for the vivid polychrome of the screen, pulpit and altar table". The rood-screen which spans the entire width of the church (it dates from 1470-80) possesses a frieze of carved vine-leaf pattern and 40 painted panels of apostles, angels and saints, including some unusual ones. We find here St Victor of Marseilles, St Simon Zelots and St Armel, monk of Brittany, who is leading a dragon by a chain.

In addition to Holy Trinity's lovely furnishings, the church is equipped with all its original fifteenth-century oak benches encased within eighteenth-century oak panelling, so forming a complete set of box pews. A long wagon roof runs uninterrupted for the entire length of the building, possibly nineteenth-century, but perfect of its kind. No less attractive is the mediaeval stained glass in the tracery lights of the aisle walls. Found nestling in the stone tracery are many exquisite and moving six-winged seraphims.

The place feels so homogeneous because it was constructed in one 20-year building campaign (1450-1470). It radiates order, purity and a kind of heraldic stillness, but it is the great sweep of the church that haunts with its grandeur and noble simplicity. This is serious architecture, and finely cared for by the Churches Conservation Trust.

TORQUAY
St John Evangelist

Montpellier Road

Difficult of access, St John's, like Butterfield's All Saints in Babbacombe, is another church in Torquay to have been designed by one of the greatest of the Victorian architects, in this case George Edmund Street. We visited it on the day of the tornado in London (7th December 2006) and the winds off the sea (the building stands high above the harbour area) were, to say the least, violent.

The church is magnificently sited, and is prominent from many angles. Its strongly featured tower with wheel tracery in the gables is best seen from across the valley, or from out at sea.

Construction spread over four campaigns: it began in 1862-3 and concluded in 1884-5, when Street's son dutifully completed the saddleback tower to his father's revised drawings of 1870. The work is singularly cohesive, splendidly proportioned and well lit, with a stately grey-stone interior remarkable for its spaciousness, nobility and richness. Every detail, down to the door hinges of the entrance porch door, was especially designed and very practical.

The nave is light, airy and tall – it is 38 feet high – with walls of a silver-grey stone with buff Ham Hill stone dressings. There is a clerestory and columns of polished Devon marble, with bands of different colours.

As a centre of nineteenth-century Anglo-Catholicism, St John's was endowed with a wealth of well-crafted fittings. There is good ironwork designed by Street (a lofty brass archway with gates and low flanking screens separating the chancel from the nave, executed by James Leaver, who also made the parclose screen), a reredos of a crucifixion scene carved by Thomas Earp, a stone pulpit and font (inlaid with marble by A. W. Blackler), an elaborate font cover by the architect's son, A. E. Street, and of particular importance two exceptionally fine stained-glass windows.

The east window from designs by Edward Burne-Jones was made by Morris & Co (1864). It represents the Church Triumphant in the Heavenly Jerusalem. The colours of this window are coolish – dark greens, lemon yellows, whites and brownish pinks. In complete contrast, the great west window (1890), also designed by Burne-Jones and executed by Morris, glows luxuriously with deep scarlets and cobalt blues. The design was based on the artist's Nine Choirs of Angels in Jesus College Chapel, Cambridge.

Facing page: Chancel arch and vaulting.

TORQUAY
St Matthew

Chelston

A suggestion by Peter Burton, who helped to edit my text, led us to this church by architects Nicholson & Corlette, hitherto unknown to us. But what a discovery! Situated in an unexceptional suburban district, St Matthew's, designed and built between 1895 and 1905, is of outstanding interest.

Its exterior, with a south-east tower, barely reveals the architectural pleasures of an Arts and Crafts interior, low and wide and built of a reddish brown Torquay red sandstone with a matching and richly carved screen (1906). Colour plays an important part in creating a mood that is warm, welcoming, domestic, and yet quietly devotional.

The interior is, as Pevsner says, of the obvious Devon type, low and wide, with viridian green painted wagon roofs with bosses. The carved arts and crafts capitals of the nave piers (there are four bays) are also delightful (see page 209), as is the most attractive font, unusually but prominently placed at the west end of the church. It is carved out of polyphant, completely smooth, and a dark grey, almost black colour, with a cover which includes a circle of kneeling angels suspended by an apparatus like a wellhead, large and unusual.

Above: Fish on capital.
Facing page: The rood-screen.

TORQUAY
Our Lady Help of Christians (R. C.)

Priory Road, St Marychurch

The pinnacled white spire of this Catholic church soars over the nearby tower of its Anglican neighbour. It dates from 1865, and is by the architect Joseph Hansom, inventor of the cab, who rather specialised in spires. Plymouth Cathedral boasts an imposing example, but the most remarkable, at 300 feet, is to be seen on his extraordinary church at Preston in Lancashire, St Walburge.

The interior of Our Lady Help of Christians also soars, to high-pointed stone-vaulted arches which inspire a sense of awe when you first enter. The two nave arcades are of different heights, the south arcade being shorter as it carries a triforium of smaller clustered arches, behind which is a broad gallery. There is much intricate stone carving: the many capitals all have realistic leaves of different trees and plants, supposedly based upon those in the garden of the church's founder and benefactor, William Potts Chatto. Relief sculptures of the Stations of the Cross line the walls of north and south aisles. There is much carving in the chancel, on the reredos and on various altars.

That all this does not seem fussy and overwhelming is partly due to the scale of the church, and partly the lack of colour (apart from the red carpet). All is creamy white limestone, which gives an ethereal lightness to this wonderful interior, and a sense of unity. The clerestory helps to light it up, and to make the vaulting part of the ensemble.

The church is the centre of a harmonious group of buildings, all by Hansom, which include a large presbytery and a former orphanage.

TOTNES

St Mary

7m/11km W of Torquay

The church is hidden from view until one comes across it off the bustling, prosperous High Street; strange, because its 120-feet tower can be seen above the town from every direction and at a considerable distance. It was constructed between 1449 and 1459, and its master mason is known – he was Roger Growdon, who had been appointed by the corporation of Totnes to add a belfry to the parish church. In the year following his appointment, Growdon and his overseers inspected steeples at Callington in Cornwall, Buckland, Tavistock and Ashburton to make a selection of the features they liked best. Three cheers for their endeavours, which resulted in a triumph. What would Totnes be today without its noble red sandstone tower?

The church itself dates from 1432 and 1460. It is a spacious and stately Perpendicular building with four aisles of five lofty bays; a town church characterised by civic grandeur and, perhaps like others of its kind, a trifle dull – or should I say complacent? The additional aisle on the north side was added as the population of the town began to expand, in 1824.

The interior has one spectacular feature: an outstandingly beautiful stone screen, which Pevsner calls "one of the most perfect in England". Carved from Beer stone in 1459-60 by order of the corporation, it runs right across the church and is continued into parclose screens to separate the north and south chancel chapels from the chancel. Regrettably, the statues of the saints in their ogee crocketed canopies all disappeared at the Reformation. No less

regrettably, G. G. Scott, Junior and Oldrid Scott saw fit to remove the screen's rood-loft during their restoration of 1867-74. One puzzles to understand why. Yet in spite of these acts of vandalism, the screen of Totnes church remains a thing of glory, and the more so on account of its colour and gilding.

Note the tomb of Christopher Blackall (d.1633) and his four wives on the wall of the north aisle, the women in long Blake-like robes. Also the gleaming brass lectern, the attractive wooden font cover, the famous 'Father' Willis organ, and the superb porch and south door with its fine carving and ironwork. The hanging brass chandelier (1701) contributes its own note of confident splendour.

Above: The four wives of Christopher Blackall.
Facing page: Candelabra, 1701.

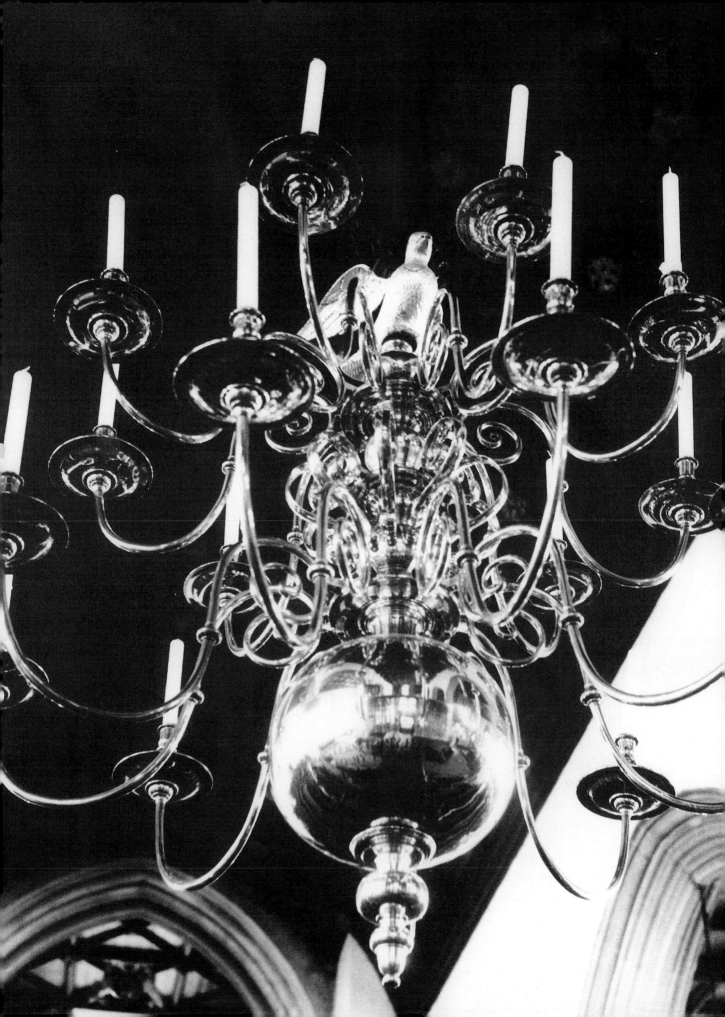

UPTON PYNE

Church of Our Lady

3m/4km N of Exeter

The church is approached up a cobbled path, across a secret, cobbled enclave edged by two cottages. Seen from here, the first glimpse is exalting. It is built of local volcanic rock (trap), blotched and mottled with a powdery whiteness. The tower, built about 1380, is embellished with statuary of an exceptionally high order. In a canopied niche on the demi-octagonal stair turret is a figure of St David, crowned and bearing a staff with a lamb at his feet. Over the west door rests a figure of Christ in Benediction.

Inside it is dark, mysterious and atmospheric; a delight for antiquarians and worshippers alike. There is a nave and two aisles, the richly textured walls of which have been coloured with an indefinable shade of dusty terracotta. The floor is flagstoned. There is some glowing glass, and old candle-holders are hanging from the roof. A little window on the right of the chancel pours light onto a white altar-cloth, like a scene in a biblical painting by Rembrandt. There are several attractive Victorian features, some dating from the restoration which took place in the nineteenth century, when the north aisle was added, and the wooden reredos. The architect was William White, who also rebuilt the chancel, added the organ chamber and provided the small arch framing his new pulpit. Perhaps a largely nineteenth-century interior, the church at Upton Pyne is nonetheless a muddled, magnificent wonder.

In the wall of the south aisle are two raised and canopied tombs of the sixteenth century. The easternmost is surmounted by the recumbent figure of a young man in armour with his sword behind him, a dog at his feet. The other is of Humphrey Larder, grandson of Edmund Larder, the figure commemorated in the other tomb.

The church guide concludes with the Churchwardens' hope that "you have enjoyed your visit to this beautiful and ancient church". I challenge anyone not to do so.

Above: King David on the stair turret of the tower.

WIDECOMBE-IN-THE-MOOR

St Pancras

5m/8km NW of Ashburton

A famous village, a honey-pot for summer tourists, and a church, the most visited in the county. The moor which surrounds it is wild and impressive, but the church, with one of Devon's proudest late Perpendicular towers, lies sheltered in a fold of hills. It is arresting from any distance.

Of early origin, the present building is of the fifteenth and sixteenth century. It has an impressive entrance with an arcaded fifteenth-century Church House in the little square that is entered through a lychgate. Its brightly lit interior with its stately arcades of granite monoliths, and white ceiled roof with painted bosses, is characterised by spaciousness. The chancel contains a number of naive bosses of great character – an angel, a Green Man (see page 228), a Pelican-in-her-Piety. The rood-screen, cut down before 1822, exhibits a fine series of early sixteenth-century paintings of saints, apostles, and the four Latin Doctors on the wainscot. Inside the tower are large and charmingly naive paintings of Moses and Aaron and four great boards with eighteenth-century lettering telling the story in vigorous rhyming couplets of how the church was struck by lightning in 1638.

On the day of our visit the building had a somewhat vacant, almost secular feeling, with visitors aimlessly shuffling around without any focus. But at other times I have been inspired by its breathless stillness.

WINKLEIGH

All Saints

10m/15km SE of Great Torrington

This is a church full of angels, heralded by one on the nave roof blowing a trumpet over the gravestones and the encircling thatched roofs (see pages 1 and 201). Visited on a bright day, it surprises with its atmosphere of glimmering splendour. The interior, sombre and brown, has the religious mood that the Victorians, especially Pugin, loved to recreate. Almost every surface is decorated: the screen with its golden cornice, the ornate chancel roof with its shield-bearing angels (carved by Harry Hems), the walls with their unusual amount of sgraffito patterns, the elaborately carved veined brown alabaster reredos, no less gorgeous. There is also a fine cradle roof over the nave (with 70 more shield-bearing angels), a sturdy polychromatic marble pulpit, and an exceptionally fine east window by Clayton and Bell. Most of these fittings were initiated, and in some cases designed, by the north Devon architect R. D. Gould in 1871-3.

The body of the church is however fifteenth century, with a stately arcade of six bays of granite piers with semi-circular arches. The glass in the tracery heads of the window at the west end of the north aisle is also mediaeval. In the well-ordered churchyard, near the south porch, grows a large Monterey cypress.

Winkleigh has great similarities with Down St Mary, another mediaeval church newly fitted out by the Gould family, using Victorian craftsmen.

Above left: Altar and reredos. Above right: Angel on chancel roof.
Facing page: Roof of north aisle chapel.

YEALMPTON
St Bartholomew

7m/11km E of Plymouth

The basin of a Norman font suggests that there has been a church on this spot for many centuries. A Cornish granite gravestone is inscribed with the words Toreus or Goreus, possibly a memorial to an ancient British chieftain who embraced Christianity 1,500 years ago.

More recent than these ancient ghosts is the church itself, distinguished by its cubic solidities, its tautness and muscularity which have rarely been surpassed. Designed by William Butterfield in (probably) 1849, it is characterised by an intelligence and clarity of proportion quite out of the ordinary. Throughout the interior (the exterior is uninteresting) there is an astonishing spatial coherence counterpointed by the dark dancing linear patterns – leaping circles in particular – inlaid onto the creamy-white walls. There is a musical movement, a harmony, a rhythm in this church. Butterfield's love of constructional polychromy is also much in evidence, particularly in his new font with its use of polished red and black Kitley marble and the chancel screen, a chunky design of purple marble with buttresses, tracery and fleurons. All this almost voluptuous richness is in contrast to the otherwise cool austerities of the interior with its springing nave arches and pale colouring. The nave's octagonal piers are composed of alternating bands of light and dark grey marble. There are clear-glass windows in the north and south aisles. The tower was added in 1915, to a design by Charles King of Plymouth.

Above: Chancel roof.
Facing page: South arcade.

OTHER
CHURCHES
TO VISIT

ABBOTS BICKINGTON

St James

8m/12km N of Holsworthy

This quiet, isolated building, approached by way of a tree-lined avenue, lies in the unspectacular countryside of north Devon which has remained relatively unchanged since the painter Turner passed this way in 1821. St James, one of the smallest churches in the county, has neither aisles nor a chancel arch, but a small south transept and western tower surmounted by a tiny spire like the tip of a dunce's cap. The east window contains some lovely jumbled fragments of fourteenth- or fifteenth-century stained glass, in which depictions of St Christopher, Christ crucified and St Anthony can be identified. There is a large number of encaustic tiles, and a charming wall monument to Thomas Pollard (d.1710), decorated with two well-fed angels wearing maroon-coloured dresses.

All those heavy of heart are recommended to visit this peaceful place and sit here for at least a quarter of an hour. Beyond the empty fields, the long line of the Dartmoor hills is visible in the distance.

ALPHINGTON

St Michael and All Angels

1m/2km SW of Exeter (virtually a suburb)

St Michael's is a Perpendicular church whose handsome tower, built of local red sandstone, is topped with limestone pinnacles. The present building, dating from around 1450, was extensively and richly restored by Hayward & Son in 1876; the east end was then rebuilt and extended. With its mediaeval chancel screen, 31 painted wainscot panels containing much original colour, wooden carved reredos (of 1901), altar-rails, parclose screen and elaborately reconstructed timber vault, this is the richest and most comely part of the interior

Alphington capitals.

– wonderful tobacco colours, chestnut and raw sienna browns.

The church possesses an exceptionally fine Norman font. It is of Beer stone with intersecting curved arches and a band of scroll roundels depicting St Michael slaying the dragon, a hunter with a bow and arrow, a man returning from hunting, and mythical beasts. Over the nave there is a barrel vault, and old tombstones set into the floor.

ASHBURTON

St Andrew

7m/11km W of Newton Abbot

The noble and commanding granite tower of St Andrew's (92 feet high) is one of the finest in the county. The large, dark interior does not live up to this proudly handsome feature. In 1882-3 it was restored by G. E. Street, who scraped the walls, added the screens and a quantity of crepuscular stained glass. The eighteenth-century brass chandeliers and brass lectern are very fine.

ASHCOMBE
St Nectan

3m/4km E of Chudleigh

Although the church lies relatively close to a busy road (the A38 from Exeter to Plymouth), it is as if it had always belonged to another time, another century.

Its exterior with coarse ribbon pointing gives no intimation of the glories that lie within. Yet one has only to open its black 'Gothic' door to enter a more sensitive world, the simple joy of a dazzling whitewashed interior lit by large clear-glassed windows.

While it is mostly Perpendicular, the mood is of the Regency, and indeed the restoration (which amounted to a rebuilding) took place between 1824-6 under the direction of Anthony Salvin, an architect renowned for his country houses, including nearby Mamhead, upon which he was working when restoring Ashcombe. Later, in the 1880s, the Norman font was removed and the mediaeval rood-screen sold. The present church is attractively bare of memorials, notices and other (all too common) visual clutter, leaving the eye free to enjoy the interior for itself.

It is indeed a charming place, at once quiet and, in its simple way, stylish. Its fifteenth-century capitals bear heraldic beasts of the Kirkhams who paid for the rebuild (see page 208), and there are tiny grotesque heads squatting on some of the bench ends. The tunnel vault over the chancel is coloured red, green and gold, and the east window, no less decorative, contains mediaeval fragments of brightly coloured glass arranged in a harlequin pattern. The window in the north aisle, dated 1885, is also handsome. Yet the glory of the church is other; it lies in its great eagle lectern dating from the time of Elizabeth I, wonderfully alert and powerful (see page 219).

On the day of our visit, the field below the church was delicately gilded with buttercups.

A black stallion stood completely still, like something in a painted illumination. Jets roared across the sky.

ASHPRINGTON
St David

4m/6km S of Totnes

The mainly fifteenth-century church (with a slim but powerful tower of earlier date) is modestly attractive; whitewashed with clear glass windows, a fine late Norman font with palmette frieze and ceiled wagon nave roof. The parclose screen by Herbert Read adds to the interior's luminous poetry.

ASHWATER
St Peter

7m/11km S of Holsworthy

Although it is not yet February, the churchyard is sprinkled with scatterings of snowdrops amongst the tombs; inside, daffodils decorate the massive Norman font. On one of its sides there is a vigorous carving of a running animal with an open crocodile-like mouth.

The interior is divided into two with an exceptionally wide nave divided from a narrower south aisle by an arcade of fourteenth- to fifteenth-century granite piers. The floor is covered with silvery slates, and there is an exciting cats-cradle of a carved wagon roof. The chancel, rebuilt in the 1880s, is unattractive.

There are nonetheless two features of exceptional charm: a large, self-confident and vigorous Royal Arms of Charles I, made of plaster and richly and brightly painted; and an ambitious stone monument to a member of the Carminow family, probably Thomas who died in 1442. His effigy lies recumbent on a tomb chest underneath an elaborate canopy, derived (Pevsner believes) from those of Bishops Branscombe and Stafford's tombs in Exeter Cathedral.

AWLISCOMBE

St Michael

2m/3km NW of Honiton

Believed to have been built on a former pagan site, the church dates from the thirteenth century, but was probably remodelled in the early sixteenth. The peace and light of the radiant north aisle is especially attractive (note here the fragments of pale mediaeval glass), but the feature most come to see is the splendid white stone screen. It has angels as corbels at the foot of the tracery, and a vine frieze in the cornice

AXMOUTH

St Michael

5m/8km W of Lyme Regis

The church contains work of almost every period from Norman (north door) to the nineteenth century (heavy font, tiled floor, pulpit, pews, etc.). Its fine tower is of the fifteenth century.

Overall the interior, restored by Hayward & Son in 1882-9, is most agreeable. There is a wide nave divided from the thirteenth-century southern aisle by Norman piers. This aisle's attractive stained-glass windows, with their representations of swallows, donkeys, a hen and her chicks are especially delightful (see page 231). They are by Bell & Son of Bristol and date from the 1890s. Prominent is the large mural monument to Hallett (1749) and a fifteenth-century painting of Christ showing His wounds.

BLACKAWTON

St Michael

5m/8km W of Dartmouth

The village lies low in the secret countryside west of Dartmouth; it is approached (like others in the South Hams) along steeply sloping deep-hedged lanes overhung with leafy branches in the summer. The church's interior, unexpectedly big, wide and handsome, possesses an exquisite sense of stillness.

It is of the fourteenth century (consecrated in 1333), greatly enlarged in the fifteenth; white painted, clear-glassed and luminous in spirit. There is a nave with two sets of four Perpendicular piers upholding a wooden barrel vault which, at different levels, extends over both aisles and chancel. The Tudor rood-screen carries the initials of Henry VIII and Katherine of Aragon, as well as carvings of Katherine's personal symbol, the pomegranate. Regrettably the coving and most of the cornice have disappeared.

The sanctuary contains a fine double piscina, one half of which was used for washing the chalice and paten, the other for washing the hands of the celebrant. Adjacent to it are equally fine sedilia. There is also a circular Norman font and a tight-laced, black wooden Jacobean pulpit.

Detail from wainscot of Blackawton screen.

Painting on the screen at Bradninch.

BRADNINCH

St Disen

5m/8km S of Cullompton

The church, dating from the fifteenth to early sixteenth century, possesses one spectacular feature: a twelve-bay rood-screen which stretches across nave and aisles. It has a fine series of early sixteenth-century wainscot paintings of prophets, apostles and other figures from the Bible (see page 227). Harry Hems considered it one of Devon's best screens (see page 226), and so it is if you ignore the slightly dead hand of its nineteenth-century restoration.

BRADSTONE

St Nonna

4m/6km SE of Launceston

This isolated church in remote country lies on the Devon side of the Tamar and relatively close to the road between Tavistock and Launceston. There is no village, but it stands beside the exuberantly conceived gatehouse of the early seventeenth-century Bradstone Manor, now a farm. The gatehouse's exciting obelisk-like pinnacles complement the octagonal pinnacles on the nearby church tower. By the roadside an alarming announcement demands attention: 'Chickens crossing'.

Dedicated to St Nonna, a Celtic saint and mother of St David, it is mostly an early sixteenth-century building, with parts dating from the eleventh or twelfth centuries. It has a fifteenth- or sixteenth-century porch (with a carved Green Man on its roof) and a nave, chancel and north aisle with wagon roofs enriched with bosses carved in foliage patterns. North of the nave is an arcade of the usual granite arches and piers with simply carved capitals. The floor is laid with large slabs of Delabole slate. The primitive male head wearing a crown or coronet that juts from the wall between two deeply set lancet windows on the south side of the chancel is of interest. Also the east window of the north aisle.

The atmosphere of this church is attractive: plain, rustic and yet elegant. Since 1996 it has been in the care of the Churches Conservation Trust.

BRATTON CLOVELLY

St Mary the Virgin

8m/12km W of Okehampton

A forgotten village in remote back lanes on the north-western edge of Dartmoor, it overlooks the valley of the Thrushel. The

Norman font at Bratton Clovelly.

church is almost entirely of late fourteenth-century date. Its interior is a complete surprise. It is loftily majestic and of almost cathedral-scale dimensions, the tower and the nave arcade of an ambition out of proportion with the current population of the parish (about 400).

The church contains many treasures – a strong Norman font of Tintagel greenstone, Perpendicular piers of polyphant stone (quarried a few miles to the west of nearby Launceston), a complete set of carved bench ends, and some interesting (but rather blotchy) seventeenth-century wall paintings. And yet I felt a trifle uncomfortable here; was there a lack of coherence in the proportions?

BRAUNTON

St Brannock

5m/8km NW of Barnstaple

The Celtic missionary-saint St Brannock founded a minster here in the sixth century, and it is probable that he is buried under the high altar. The immediate setting of the present church, with its big Norman tower, monumental buttresses and silvery lead-covered spire, is a delight: a large churchyard, the loveliest of lime avenues and a group of pastel-painted vernacular houses. Yet most of the 'village' of Braunton, the largest in Devon, is well advanced in its suburbanisation.

The interior, resembling a great hall, is an impressive space, yet somehow secular rather than sacred in feeling. There is an aisleless nave of exceptional width (34 feet) covered by a massive dark brown wagon roof. It is on the gloomy, even mournful, side, with deeply-set window splays (from which the plaster has been removed) and some unforgivable modern stained glass. On the other hand, the church possesses an extensive series of bench ends dating from 1560 and 1593, an early chancel screen, some good Jacobean woodwork, a number of roof bosses, (including one of a pig feeding a litter) and a selection of dour grey wall monuments to the local gentry.

BRENTOR
St Michael-of-the-Rock

5m/8km N of Tavistock

The position of this parish church is spectacular. It is situated about 30 feet high on the edge of an isolated volcanic rock rising sheer out of the barely less dramatic Dartmoor landscape, wild and open to the sky. It can be seen for miles around. It is dedicated to St Michael, the angel of high places, who is said to have landed on the nearest high point whenever he visited the Earth.

To reach the church you must walk (or drive) across the moor, sparkling this May day with great bushes of gorse aflame with cadmium yellow flowers. Then, slowly climbing for over a mile you reach the car park from which the final ascent must be made – the aged, the infirm and the tired are not advised to continue much further. The tor is 1,130 feet high with spectacular views from its summit. On a clear day Plymouth Sound can be seen.

How early this site was used is not known. The first record of its existence is of before 1150, and in the thirteenth century it belonged to Tavistock Abbey, which established an annual fair on the site. It is a small church; a nave and chancel only, with a low battlemented tower built of volcanic stone quarried on the hill. The interior is tiny and plain, with a low shallow-pitched wooden roof, and simple chunky wooden pews, which must date from the late nineteenth-century restoration. The tower may have been added early in the fourteenth century, as Bishop Stapledon came to consecrate the church on 4th December 1319. Imagine his vestments furling in the

Below and facing page: St Michael-of-the-Rock, Brentor.

wind. A later visitor, the antiquarian Tristram Risdon, wrote in 1625 that it was "a church full bleak and weather beaten, all alone, as if it were forsaken."

BRIDFORD
St Thomas a Becket

4m/6km E of Moretonhampstead

This all-granite church is an early fourteenth-century building, reconstructed c.1500. Its chief glory is its wonderful sixteenth-century eight-bay rood-screen, believed to date from 1508. The rood-loft and coving may be missing, but what survives is an exceptionally lavish, splendidly coloured and well preserved screen. There are pomegranates and gourds, and on the wainscoting a series of small carved figures some eight inches high, all retaining some of their original colouring. Both ecclesiastics and laymen are represented, even the odd jester, but their faces have been cut away by the Puritan soldiery stationed in the village preparatory to meeting their Royalist adversaries at Heathfield.

Dartmoor is visible from the village.

Painting of the back of the screen at Bridford.

BROADCLYST
St John the Baptist

5m/8km NE of Exeter

The size of the church reflects the wealth of this enormous parish, the second largest in Devon. It dates from the Perpendicular period, and has a wonderful tower completed in the sixteenth century, similar to the one at Cullompton but less ostentatious, more austere. Church, churchyard, tower and Red Lion Inn make a picturesque group. Peter De Wint would have enjoyed painting them and, I don't doubt, staying in the Inn.

The interior is spacious but overpowered by its Victorian stained glass. There are four handsome tombs, the finest of which is that to Sir Roger de Nonant, whose family were Norman squires in the village; he lies uncomfortably recumbent in armour within the sedilia. More sumptuous, if too elaborate, is the memorial to Sir John Acland who died in 1620, the first member of that family to settle in Broadclyst. Erected in his lifetime, it is overcrowded with Jacobean decoration – strapwork, cartouches, fruit and putti. The beautiful and unusual fourteenth-century tracery (but not the glass) of the window in the north aisle, and the carved angels of the nave arches are certainly worth discovering.

BROOKING
St Barnabus

3m/4km W of Totnes

Although the name of the Victorian architect of this smallish church is unknown, it possesses a confident authority quite out of the ordinary (could it even be by Pearson, who designed nearby Landscove?). There is a slender, needling, broach-spire and in contrast to its sombre grey exterior, a surprising creamy Caen stone interior. This contains not only strongly chamfered

View through to the chancel at St Barnabus, Brooking.

window recesses and arches in the Early English style, but two massive arcade piers of polished charcoal-grey marble to the south aisle. The attractive but slightly mechanical corbel carvings, and the glass by Hardman (east window) and by Clayton and Bell (south aisle west window) are definitely worth noting. The church dates from 1850-5, and enjoys a most amiable atmosphere.

On the day of my visit, the rooks nesting in the huge trees surrounding the spire were making their presence strongly felt.

BRUSHFORD
St Mary the Virgin

4m/6km SW of Winkleigh

I visited this remote little building on a hot afternoon in early spring. The churchyard grass glowed with primroses and the surrounding countryside brimmed with light and fertility. The church stands alone in a field, surrounded by tall trees. There is no village.

The stumpy early sixteenth-century tower is unusual. It has a weather-boarded top and a charming slated steeple, but the interior,

thoroughly restored in 1876, is not exciting.

There is a simple Norman door which opens into the nave, and a wagon roof with bosses which include a Tudor rose and the pomegranate device of Katherine of Aragon. The rood-screen, with panels filled up with filigree tracery, has similarities to the one at nearby Coldridge. There are stiff Victorian pews and, standing on the floor, three mediaeval bells.

BUCKERELL
St Mary & St Giles

3m/4km W of Honiton

A small, unassuming early mediaeval church in a remote parish (population 270) in the Otter valley, it has transepts and no aisles, but a west tower. The interior is pleasingly intimate, but without notable features except for an attractive traceried screen (brought here from another church), some plain eighteenth-century box pews, and Victorian light fittings. There is a gallery at the west end of the nave, and some unpretentious memorials: one to the memory of Admiral Samuel Graves, by the sculptor John Bacon in 1792, and a neo-classical tablet to Elizabeth Graves, 1767.

BUCKLAND MONACHORUM
St Andrew

4m/6km S of Tavistock

A large granite church with an ambitious but curiously unexciting interior: a complete Perpendicular rebuilding of an earlier structure restored in 1869. In fact, everything is here: good fifteenth-century windows, a fine five-bay arcade, a rich ceiled wagon roof, a big Perpendicular font, carved oak figures of angels each playing different musical instruments, etc., but some quality of vitality seems to be missing.

However, the most sensational feature is the south chancel aisle, the Drake aisle, which contains two remarkable monuments, both by John Bacon. One, huge, white and classical, is the Heathfield monument of 1795. This commemorates Lord Heathfield, the Admiral who successfully defended Gibraltar against the Spanish from 1783 to 1799. An allegorical figure, possibly Britannia, holds up the arms of Gibraltar (see page 223), and a putto holds the key of the fortress in his hand. Background reliefs show a sea battle with a ship on fire, and a kiln for making cannonballs. The other monument is dedicated to Sir Francis Henry Drake.

BURLESCOMBE
St Mary

5m/8km SW of Wellington

St Mary's lies in undulating countryside close to the M5, and therefore in a landscape slightly soiled by 'development'. The building originates from the fourteenth century, and has a tall interior, short, wide and with generous proportions. There are three wagon roofs and an arcade of elegant whitish Beer stone piers. Also two good wall monuments to the Ayshfords of Ayshford, some insipid Victorian glass and a late Perpendicular tomb chest with some original colour.

BURRINGTON
Holy Trinity

4m/6km NW of Chulmleigh

The church is of early sixteenth-century date with dark brown unceiled wagon roofs to the nave and south aisle, the latter with 38 angel figures bearing shields. There is an arcade of five bays with granite piers and four traceried Dartmoor granite windows in the south aisle. The most attractive feature is the nave's coloured eight-bay rood-screen, complete with three strips of ornament and cresting, decorated with carvings of flowers between the ribs of the coving. A heavy mediaeval door, some seventeenth-century communion rails and a handsome Norman font (which the guide states has been in use for 32 generations) complete the special features of this otherwise dullish interior, restored by John Haywood in 1869.

CADELEIGH
St Bartholomew

4m/6km SW of Tiverton

My approach was a spectacular example of the hazards and delights of a church crawl. Travelling between Crediton and Tiverton, I turned off towards Cadeleigh to descend an extremely steep hill overhung by branches and the lacy flowers of cow parsley, further closing the route. Then up the other side (altitudes rising steeply here, attaining 770 feet), with quick glimpses of the rounded hills seen between the gaps in the luxuriant foliage.

St Bartholomew's stands on this eminence overlooking views of some of Devon's most beautiful countryside. It is approached up a cobbled path and through a porch. Its interior, medium-sized and unpretentious, has an attractive simplicity: nave and aisle separated by a five-bay arcade, dark brown box pews, sage green wagon roofs (with simple bosses) and white plastered walls.

Within seconds of entering your eye is caught by a distant sensation – the Leach memorial, according to Pevsner the largest of its type in any Devon church (see page 221). It fills part of the north aisle and was erected c.1630 by Sir Simon Leach in memory of his second wife, Katherine Tuberville. The sculpture shows both figures (recumbent), his son and daughter-in-law (kneeling) and the usual accompaniment of little children, within an elaborate architectural framing of coffered arch, broken pediment and columns. Pevsner writes that the whole is "grand, but not sculpturally accomplished", which by the highest standards is certainly true, except that I found it a delightful, even poetic monument, well worth the effort required to visit this remote and thinly populated village.

CHAGFORD
St Michael the Archangel

4m/6km NW of Moretonhampstead
Chagford is an ancient stannary town on the edge of Dartmoor, now enjoying an obvious prosperity. There is a central 'Square' and, close by, an extensive churchyard and early fifteenth-century granite church. The tower was completed in 1513.

In 1865 there was a restoration of the interior. The old high pews were removed, as were the wall plaster and the north and south chancel screens. In 1888 the sanctuary was decorated by J. L. Pearson in what Pevsner describes as a totally un-Devonian way, but with a handsome reredos – a triptych in Quattrocento Italian style. In the north and south aisles between 1884 and 1908 new windows were installed; these make for a very gloomy interior. The rood-loft and screen, in a traditional style, date from 1927; the monument to Sir John Whiddon, from 1575.

CHAWLEIGH
St James

2m/3km SE of Chulmleigh
This church, including its slim, rather Cornish tower, appears to have been completely rebuilt in the fifteenth century. It has a broad and spacious interior, a ceremonial granite arcade, clear-glass windows and a blue-coloured chancel roof. The rood-screen, although heavily restored, provides a handsome effect. There are two

robust wall monuments, one of which, to George Radford, dated 1667, is particularly fine.

Before leaving the village, note the attractive ensemble of tower, lychgate, former Church house and school.

Detail of monument at St James's, Chawleigh.

CHELDON
St Mary

8m/12km S of South Molton
A late discovery, almost dismissed by Pevsner, but a moving place: small, countrified and poetic. Here in this remote landscape above the wooded valley of the Little Dart, small congregations have gathered for centuries to worship and give praise. Today, although services are held but once a month, the empty church can yet bring a visitor to his or her knees.

The setting is memorable; a scatter of gravestones, a stout brown tower and a handsome Perpendicular window in the south wall. The interior is homely and mediaeval. There is a ceiled wagon roof to the chancel,

Metal screen at St Mary's, Cheldon.

fifteenth-century bench ends, an eighteenth-century pulpit, altar-rails, and a surprising and stately metal gilded screen made out of two mace rests dated 1737 and 1743. I had a sense that the screen and the two unexplained putti on the window sills gave this otherwise modest interior a quietly unaffected aristocratic mood. Before leaving, note the floor which leads from the porch to the nave; generations of feet have worn down the stone but left the carved edges in good condition.

To obtain entry I had called on the help of Terry Pinchombe, keyholder, local farmer and a churchwarden for 41 years. Talking with him I could see how his character, direct and simple, was true not only to the values which underpinned his church but to the old rural culture itself. This was an economy directly founded on the land, on thrift and skill, and on people's competence to take care of themselves. Oliver Goldsmith described it well:

A time there was, ere England's griefs began,
When every rood of ground maintain'd its man;

For him light labour spread its wholesome store,
Just gave what life requir'd, but gave no more;
His best companions, innocence and health,
And his best riches, ignorance of wealth.

CHERITON BISHOP
St Mary

6m/10km SW of Crediton
The church has a good collection of fittings: a Norman font, a sixteenth-century pulpit, a coloured mediaeval rood-screen with traces of the original gilding and, over the south door, a rare Elizabethan painted Royal Arms. An appealing interior, but not exceptional.

CHITTLEHAMPTON
St Hieritha

5m/8km W of South Molton
The Celtic saint Hieritha, usually known as St Urith, was born at East Stowford, near Barnstaple, in the 7th century. Little is known of her life. She was a consecrated virgin, presumably a hermit, and was cut down by scythes yielded by local (apparently female) haymakers at the instigation of a jealous, possibly pagan, stepmother. It is told that where she fell, bleeding and in pain, a spring of water gushed forth out of the earth.

Urith was buried in the church, where over the centuries her shrine became extremely popular with both local people and the many pilgrims from afar who sought to find renewal at this sacred place. It has been believed that it was their offerings that enabled what is perhaps Devon's finest tower to be built; but another suggestion relates a completely different story: it was a gift of the sixteenth-century absentee vicar, Richard Woolman.

Whatever the truth, in 1539, as at other pilgrimage centres, the cult of St Urith was suppressed, the shrine closed and her statue removed and probably destroyed. Yet even today, the shadow of St Urith survives; every summer – on 8th July, to be precise – after a procession through the village, children lay posies of flowers to bless her holy well. According to Hoskins, writing in the 1950s, the Christian name of Urith or Hieritha continued to be bestowed on daughters born in the neighbourhood, but the present incumbent, Rev. Davis, tells me that the tradition is no longer observed.

The tower is famous for its height and elegance: it rises with splendour above the modest cottages surrounding three sides of the village's gently sloping square. Beautifully proportioned, of four stages, it reaches a height of 125 feet including its eight soaring crocketed pinnacles The exterior of the church, of Perpendicular design (c.1470-1520), is broadly worthy of this feature, but the interior, restored in 1872, comes as something of a disappointment. Its plasterwork has been removed, leaving prominently pointed lead-coloured walls. By the nineteenth century, the rubblestone walls of many churches which had been rendered on the inside with years of successive coats of plaster were scraped to the stone – an exercise William Morris (see page 245) described as "skinning a church alive".

There is a late mediaeval pulpit (c.1500) whose carving is rather cabbagey. In the north transept is a fine monument to John Gifford and family.

A pleasing feature is the French-style pleached avenue of trees leading from the village square to the church porch.

CHULMLEIGH
St Mary Magdalene

8m/12km S of South Molton
The quiet town of Chulmleigh is one of the most attractive in north Devon. Its church is large and has a commandingly proud tower, which can be seen to advantage from the Little

Dart valley and the road from Chawleigh. Its largely fifteenth-century interior is nicely proportioned and has Perpendicular windows. There is a 51-foot rood-screen, a wagon roof with many bosses and 38 small carved wooden angels supporting it.

CLOVELLY
All Saints

9m/15km W of Bideford
This church lies close to Clovelly Court and in sight of today's milky cobalt-coloured sea. Inside are the memorials of seven Carys, from Robert (c.1457-1540), to another Robert (1697-1724), who died childless; they include one to George Cary (1543-1601), whose enterprise put Clovelly on the map. A later monument is to Charles Kingsley, father of the author of *Westward Ho!*.

The Norman foundation was enlarged in the Perpendicular period, when the north wall was replaced by an arcade of four bays and a north aisle. Architecturally, All Saints may not have an exceptional interior, but it has a handsome, cared-for feeling and a sense of warm-hearted timeless devotion. The surrounding graveyard, with its slate tombstones to generations of Clovelly parishioners, is exceptionally attractive (see page 210).

COLEBROOKE
St Andrew

1m/2km SW of Cullompton
The scattered village stands high on the south side of the valley of a tributary of the river Yeo. The church tower stands even higher, a commanding presence. Its interior is airy and spacious, with white piers and arches and pink walls reminiscent of a birthday cake. But the most striking feature is the mannered but beautiful parclose screen on its south and west sides. This is thought to date from the

Facing page: Chittlehampton tower.

early sixteenth century, and its workmanship is exceptional, Franco-Flemish rather than English. A carver from Brittany has been suggested. Also exceptional are the unusually vigorous carvings of a wild man and a fool on the prayer desk in the chancel, which seem to belong to a fairy-tale. Their authorship is unknown, but there are few, if any, living sculptors whose work can match their imaginative power.

COLLATON ST MARY
St Mary the Virgin

On W edge of Paignton
This church, the vicarage and school were built by a Mr and Mrs J. R. Hodge in memory of their daughter Mary who died in 1864. Designed by J. W. Rowell, it is worthy of a

visit, if only to admire its excellent furnishings and glass by J. F. Bentley, the architect of Westminster Cathedral. There is a remarkable font and wooden cover, pulpit, chandelier and carved reredos based on Leonardo's *Last Supper*. This is a building without the least trace of pretension, characterised by a touching simplicity and devotion. It is not in the same league as Devon's grandest churches, but charms with its modesty.

COMBE MARTIN
St Peter ad Vincula

4m/6km E of Ilfracombe
One of the best churches of the neighbourhood, writes Pevsner, and this is certainly true of its magnificent tower. It is 99 feet high and has tall, thin, crocketed

Bench ends at St Andrew's, Colebrooke.

Facing page: 18th-century screen at Holy Cross, Cruwys Morchard.

pinnacles. Seen from Knap Down, where you look down on the village, it is of a memorable nobility. The interior is less inspiring; even leaden, but with some attractive features such as its fifteenth-century rood-screen with painted figures, and the Early Renaissance Florentine-style monument to Judith Hancock who died in 1634. There are old choir stalls topped with a lizard and a dolphin, as well as a less than remarkable stained-glass window of modern design.

CRUWYS MORCHARD
Holy Cross

5m/8km W of Tiverton

As soon as you enter this church, you encounter a wonderful eighteenth-century font cover, shaped like an onion dome, with a life-size dove hovering above (see page 214). Look down the nave, and you see the other great treasure, a classical Georgian screen, like the façade of a temple, with fluted Corinthian columns and a pediment. It encloses an intimate chancel with Jacobean communion rails on three sides. There are box pews for the local farmers' families, a plain plastered barrel-vaulted ceiling and a monument to John Avery of 1695. The general mood of this interior, calm and serious, is more like that of a library than a church.

The setting is one of great charm. There is no village, the centre of the parish is the church, and the manor house has been the seat of the Cruwys family since the reign of King John. Opposite the white-painted revolving lychgate there is a handsome park of old trees which gives the feeling, as does the church, of the atmosphere of a less stressful age. Constable could have painted these trees, and Kilvert have worshipped in the church.

DARTINGTON
St Mary

2m/3km NW of Totnes

The original parish church adjacent to Dartington Hall was pulled down in 1873 (apart from its tower) and rebuilt about a mile away beside the turning to the Hall off the A384. The original font, altar, pulpit, porch vaulting and restored screen were installed in the new building, whose ground plan is of the same dimensions as the mediaeval church. The ancient door, with patches of red paint remaining, is also original.

The Beer stone arcades from the old church were re-erected, but on Portland stone bases to make them loftier. The church has a stately tower topped by traceried battlements and long pinnacles. An outstanding feature. The east window by Clayton and Bell is from their best period (see page 233).

The architect was J. L. Pearson, whose design, although characterised by richness and an airy space, feels here just a little academic.

Crossing arcade and organ at St Mary's, Dartington.

St Petrox, Dartmouth, behind Dartmouth Castle.

DARTMOUTH

St Petrox

7m/11km SE of Totnes

The setting of this seventeenth-century church in the Gothic style is a spectacular one. It lies adjacent to Dartmouth Castle, dramatically sited under a steep and wooded hillside rising from the west bank of the Dart estuary, just before it joins the sea. This site is about a mile from the town.

A record of 1192, referring to it as "the monastery of St Peter," suggests that this is an old foundation, but the present church dates from 1641-2. It has a fine if rather dour exterior, but an interior which is slightly disappointing. There is a plain plastered barrel vault overarching a wide nave, separated from its two aisles by an arcade of octagonal piers.

There are three seventeenth-century brasses (under a carpet at the east end of the building), hatchments, a circular Norman font, a seventeenth-century pulpit and several prominent charity boards. The mood is secular and subdued on account of the semi-opaque glass which fills the windows.

DITTISHAM

St George

3miles/4km SE of Totnes

One spectacular feature characterises the interior - not its good early fifteenth-century screen with painted panels, nor its barrel roof, Norman font, Royal Coat of Arms of Charles II, nor the stained glass supposedly designed by Pugin, all delightful – but its marvellous fifteenth-century pulpit carved out of stone.

The sides of this incomparable object are decorated with five canopied niches divided by vertical shafts ornamented with lusty foliage, vine stems and grapes. In the niches stand the stiffly standing figures of saints or apostles.

From a sophisticated viewpoint – and Pevsner has described the carving of this pulpit as "very crude" – the carving and painting (red, white, gold, ultramarine) is rough, but that for me is its unaffected charm. It has the haunting power of a Scottish ballad or a Devon folksong. The best of the county's indigenous art, as we can see it in this pulpit, combines a sensuous sweetness with a luxuriant magnificence. Contemplating this pulpit, you can get no closer to the mystical but bucolic spirit of the Middle Ages.

Then leave the church and look across its graveyard, the long silvery grass blowing in the wind. Look to the roofs of a few distant cottages, the wooded hillsides, and down below the gleaming river Dart. Seeing all this, and the pulpit in the church, is compelling reason for a visit to Dittisham.

DODDISCOMBSLEIGH

St Michael

6m/10km SW of Exeter

Hidden away and difficult to find, St Michael's lacks distinction save for its remarkable late fifteenth-century stained glass, predominantly white and creamy in colour but sometimes enlivened by sudden clashes of scarlet and strong ultramarine. The general effect, if not robust, is sensitive and poetic. The figures represented are the saints and the Virgin (see pages 230 and 231).

The east window is the most remarkable. It shows the Seven Sacraments – mass, marriage, confirmation, penance, ordination, baptism and extreme unction – and includes a Blake-like figure of Christ, apparently supplied during restoration by Clayton and Bell in 1879.

DOWLAND

St Peter

7m/11km SE of Torrington

Turning the large cold key in the lock, slowly pushing open the church door, I catch glimpses of the interior through the widening gap (see page 120). Yes, even before I've entered the building I know that this is the kind of place that I especially love. Here one encounters the old Devon.

The interior is plastered throughout and, on the morning of my visit, great blades of honeyed light marked the whitewashed plaster and gleamed upon the woodwork. The surface of things had a marvellous enrichment.

There is a north aisle divided from the nave by an unusual arcade of oak arches and pillars (c.1500), the loveliest mediaeval ceiled wagon roofs, slate floors, a complete set of carved bench ends with decorative tracery, and a bell-chamber with hanging ropes. In the sanctuary are finely lettered floor slabs to the Staffords of nearby Stafford Barton.

The churchyard is also attractive with a plain fifteenth-century tower, a miscellaneous collection of gravestones, and a low, thatched Church House on its perimeter.

There are two services a month, with a regular attendance of between ten and twelve people.

DOWN ST MARY

St Mary the Virgin

7m/11km NW of Crediton

An unexpectedly rich interior, with burnished glints of brass in the darkness. Although its west tower, a landmark, is mediaeval, and the building itself belongs to the twelfth century, its furnishings are basically a Victorian achievement and one of the most remarkable in the county. Under the aegis of the Rev. W. T. A. Radford, the church

Detail of the screen at St Michael and All Angels, Dunchideock.

was progressively remodelled by a succession of eminent architects and designers. In 1848, John Hayward rearranged the choir; in 1866, G. E. Street designed the reredos and sanctuary enrichments, with carving by Thomas Earp and mosaics by Salviati. The nave and aisle were rebuilt in 1870-2 by John F. Gould, who also designed the wonderful brass and iron pulpit. The eight-bay rood-screen, closely modelled on late mediaeval precedents, was begun in 1881 by the village carpenters, the father and son team of William and Zachariah Buchell.

The stained glass is also remarkable. The east window of 1854 is by one of the most eminent of the nineteenth-century glass makers, John Hardman; the rest of the glass, variously dated, is by Clayton and Bell.

No less noteworthy are the finely carved late mediaeval bench ends; the rich fifteenth-century barrel vault; the communion rails of brass and iron set with agates and cornelians, the charming pulpit stairs and, unforgettably, the twelfth-century carved tympanum in the south porch, which illustrates Daniel in the lion's den. Its archaic spirit, raw and mythic like the pulpit at Luppitt, comes from a different world from the interior's mystic richness, conjured up by some of the most talented decorators of the nineteenth century.

DUNCHIDEOCK
St Michael and All Angels

4m/6km SW of Exeter
Although the church is close to Exeter, it is tucked away among the foothills of Haldon and feels isolated and remote; it is certainly difficult to discover, but worth the effort. Its red sandstone exterior (with slim west

tower) is beautiful seen against the luminous golden fawns of the shaven cornfields and the dark almost black colours of the surrounding trees.

The interior is intimate, not to say cosy, and most attractive; a charming country church. The overpowering impression is of wood: chocolate-brown wagon roofs; nut-coloured and tobacco-brown pews (some with carved bench ends) and an exceptionally handsome fifteenth-century rood-screen (restored by Herbert Read in 1893) complete with doors, groining and cornice. The rood itself is modern, but note the fabulous intricacy of the carving which encases one of the nave piers, and the charming stained-glass windows in the chancel. Take delight, too, in the old oil lamps, whose retention is usually a sign of sensitive care.

EAST BUDLEIGH

All Saints

2m/3km N of Budleigh Salterton
East Budleigh is a comfortable village with many thatched cob cottages. The church, built of red sandstone, is largely fifteenth-century. It has a spacious interior with a stately four-bay Beer stone arcade, one pier on the south side with a capital of a Green Man. It also has a most wonderful collection of 63 bench ends carved in 1537 with motifs such as a ship (East Budleigh was once a port), sheep shears, coats of arms (including those of Sir Walter Raleigh, who was born in the village), angels and what looks like an alligator or crocodile. There is a fairly simple fifteenth-century screen, a stone font and some Perpendicular windows filled with Victorian and later glass of a higher than average quality. The window representing the Garden of Eden is particularly attractive.

EGGESFORD

All Saints

2m/3km S of Chulmleigh
The entry is a coup de théâtre. As you open the door, a spotlight illuminates the full-size honey-coloured standing figure of Arthur, Viscount Chichester, greeting you from the opposite wall, his two wives recumbent and golden on either side of him, his seven diminutive children lined up glumly at his feet. The composition, eccentric in itself, is the more so when we learn that it was raised in 1650, 25 years before the Viscount's death.

Two other monuments include that to Edward, Viscount Chichester and his wife, stiffly lying side by side as they have done since 1648. The other, if less flamboyant (yet severe to the point of theatricality), is for William Fellowes, Esq., who bought the property in 1718. It is a richly handsome classical ensemble of varied grey and black marbles dating from 1723. On the day of my last visit, the cool colours of the monument were complemented by a gorgeous arrangement of orange and maroon fruits and flowers.

Today it has the feel of a cheery mausoleum, or the private chapel of the big house which, before its reconstruction on a new site, originally stood only a few yards away. Thereafter All Saints has had an eventful history. In 1867, it was completely restored and much rebuilt, but in the eighties of the last century, it was made redundant – its congregation had dwindled to four people and it needed an enormous sum of money for its repair. Nonetheless – and this is probably Devon's most inspiring restoration story – the launch of a successful campaign led to its repair and reopening. Today, a service is held once every month, attended by a congregation of 18 to 24 people.

The monument to Arthur, Viscount Chichester at All Saints, Eggesford.

EXETER
St Michael

Dinham Road

The soaring spire, 220 feet high and modelled on that of Salisbury, is a major landmark of the city, even though the church, exploiting its site on a bluff above the Exe, lies on the periphery of its central area.

Built in 1865-8 by Rhode Hawkins (and financed by William Gibbs of Tyntesfield, whose effigy lies on the north side of the sanctuary), the architecture of St Michael's reflects that of the Camden Society and the architect Pugin.

It has a long and impressive five-bay nave with clerestoried windows, passage aisles, an elaborate chancel, and, at its west end, a richly coloured rose window. Decoration was influenced, it seems, by William Butterfield who was building All Saints, Babbacombe at the time. There are grotesque animals in the spandrels of the arcades and angels on the screen at the west end of the nave. Arthur Blomfield designed the font (1885), and Caröe the reredos.

The scale of this building is awesome, the mood extravagant, severe and, for me, rather cold-hearted. But if I did not love this building, I was certainly impressed by it.

Peregrine falcons settled on the tower in 1987 and have been breeding there since 1998.

Do not miss the delightful precinct of Tudor-style almshouses, Exeter Free Cottages, at the back of the church. These were also paid for by William Gibbs and built in 1862.

EXWICK
St Andrew

1m/2km NW of Exeter

On its completion in 1842, *The Ecclesiologist* pronounced St Andrew's "the best specimen of the modern church we have seen". The architect was John Hayward of Exeter, at the beginning of his long career. According to Paul Joyce, the significance of this building lies in the fact that it was the first example of the application of Pugin's principles to an Anglican church.

In 1873-5, again under Hayward, the north aisle was added, the chancel lengthened and the interior delightfully redecorated. Many fittings remain. These include the stone font, altar and reredos (which accommodates a mosaic of the Ascension of Christ by Salviati), a carved pulpit, an unusually attractive east window (by William Wailes of Newcastle), a richly painted ceiling, altar-rails, and decorative Victorian tile flooring. Regrettably some of the chancel's original mural paintings were overpainted in, I believe, the 1970s. Although small, St Andrew's is one of Devon's most attractive nineteenth-century churches, and deserves to be better known.

Stag drinking. Carving on the altar at St Andrew's, Exwick.

FARRINGDON
St Petrock

3m/4km E of Exeter

Perhaps not everyone would like this church. Hoskins found it 'hideous'. But for me it was a special and unexpected delight, the perfect example of what a country church could (and should) be like. Small in scale, domestic in atmosphere, unpretentious but modestly distinguished as far as its architecture is concerned, St Petrock's should be seen.

Angel and painted flowers at St Petrock, Farringdon.

Rebuilt in 1870-1 by William White, re-using as much of the original mediaeval material as possible, it has an un-Devonian boldly louvered belfry and broach-spire. Warm and homely, its interior is faced throughout with brick from the nearby Woodbury works. Local Heavitree sandstone and Dartmoor granite have also been employed and, adding a further intimacy to the church, some of the walls have been sensitively stencilled by an incumbent's wife.

Like Upton Pyne, also restored by William White, St Petrock's is a delightful place, alive with small touches of invention.

GITTISHAM
St Michael

2m/3km SW of Honiton

An attractive church in an idyllically pretty village of cob and thatched cottages which appears to have remained unchanged for centuries. St Michael's has white painted plaster walls, a number of clear-glass windows, box pews, a gallery, and an atmosphere of warmth, civility and charm. The keynote here is comfort.

There are several interesting monuments. One is of alabaster and two types of marble, for two stocky and all-too-real Elizabethans, both at prayer, but in all probability more attentive to the mundane than the celestial. But who knows what is passing through the heads of Henry Beaumont and his wife Joanne, who died in 1627? Or through the minds of the figures in another much grander monument: Lady (Ursula) and Sir Thomas Putt? Well, it's obvious from the evidence of their frigid and preposterous monument that they were both vain and proud. "Cold, competent, expensive, and metropolitan", writes Pevsner, unable to resist the temptation to criticise their monument. Vastly more attractive is the stained-glass east window of the Ascension of Christ by Heaton, Butler & Baynes (1873), and a charming painting of King David with his harp (1744) at the back of the church.

On the occasion of our visit, the lovely, honeyed light of evening lay upon the floors. The views of the wooded landscape beyond the churchyard are very beautiful.

St David playing the harp, St Michael's, Gittisham.

HALBERTON

St Andrew

3m/4km E of Tiverton

Halberton village lies in undulating countryside close to the Grand Western Canal. The church is in the centre of the village, but is tucked away close to the active National school. It is a large building of red sandstone with a tall tower and an early fourteenth-century nave. There is a Norman font, the bowl with three scollops on each side, a fine mediaeval pulpit, a wooden barrel vault and an extensive and finely carved early-fifteenth-century screen. The church is well cared for, pleasant, but somewhat impersonal in mood.

HARBERTON

St Andrew

2m/3km SW of Totnes

At first sight, seen against the sky, standing nobly on a steeply rising hillside, the church at Harberton lifts the heart. Its 78-feet high tower, although similar to other Perpendicular ones, feels especially enspiriting. The view from its porch is also a delight – an unspoilt green landscape of rising hills and grazing sheep with barely a house in sight. The vaulting and eight bosses of the two-storeyed fourteenth-century porch are especially handsome. A family of swallows had wisely chosen to make it their home.

The interior does not maintain this degree of excitement. The great north and south aisle windows and the nave piers (completed c.1370) are certainly stately, but the well intentioned Victorian additions which darken the church, and especially its chancel, are unfortunate. Nineteenth-century stained-glass may be wonderful, but has a tendency to be academic and unmoving, as it is here. The very fine screen was blemished when a Victorian 'restorer' saw fit to touch it up with paint in what can only be called a hurdy-gurdy style. At the same time (1861) sheets of tin were inserted in the panels of the wainscot and new picture-book-style figures painted on them (some of the original panels are on display in the north aisle).

Nonetheless, there are some splendours: a fine Norman red sandstone font, and an especially resplendent carved and painted fifteenth-century stone pulpit characterised by bucolic vitality. There is also the Royal Arms of Queen Anne (1702-14), and of special note a life-size marble monument to Tito, the lamented son of Sir Robert and Lady Harvey, who died while still at school as a boy of ten. His figure was carved in alabaster in 1895, and its loving spirit and poignant tenderness (see page 220)go a long way to redeeming the chill professionalism of the stained glass. In the graveyard is the white marble Harvey mausoleum of 1895.

Looking into the bell chamber, St Petroc's, Harford.

HARFORD
St Petroc

2m/3km N of Ivybridge

The church of this sparsely populated parish on the southern fringe of Dartmoor is peaceful, unpretentious and spare. Pevsner calls it a humble church, and so it is. St Petroc's stands almost alone beside the Erme where it leaves the moor, and has an exterior as venerable as a fairy tale.

It is a granite building of the late fifteenth to the early sixteenth century, a simple form of Perpendicular style, largely (and successfully) rebuilt in 1883-4. The rood-screen at some date having being removed, there is no structural division between chancel and nave. There are good late seventeenth-century altar-rails, a handsome, sturdy pulpit, ceiled wagon roofs, and two good monuments, one to an Elizabethan Speaker of the House of Commons. In the churchyard a cross restored in memory of the Rev. Augustus Toplady (d.1778), Vicar of Harford and author of the hymn *Rock of Ages*.

On the day of our visit, the altar with its shiny brass candlesticks, communion plate and lectern was decorated with moorland flowers, their woody fragrance permeating the church. Outside, a wind was blowing hard.

HENNOCK
St Mary

3m/4km N of Bovey Tracey

The village of Hennock is approached through deep-set, narrow lanes. Churchwardens of its fifteenth-century, fully-aisled granite church were preparing for a funeral on the morning of our visit.

The simple but attractive whitewashed interior contains a screen with early-sixteenth-century paintings of saints and apostles, a Norman font, ceiled wagon roofs and some mediaeval glass – but much is said

to have been carted away at the restoration of 1874-5. The glory of this church is its painted celure above the rood-screen: a broad band of dusky ultramarine studded with golden stars – it is astonishing.

Leaving the church, we passed fields white with frost. A powerful golden sun shone in a clear blue sky.

The celure at St Mary's, Hennock.

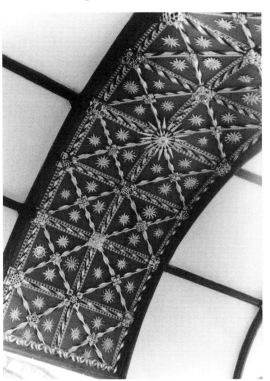

HIGH BICKINGTON
St Mary

7m/11km E of Torrington

It is a twelfth-century building enlarged in the early fourteenth and again in the early sixteenth centuries, with a thinnish, Cornish-type Perpendicular tower. There is a Norman doorway with some zigzag decoration of the arches.

But it is the bench ends that one comes to see. There are about 70 dating from around 1500-30: pairs of saints or prophets, instruments of the Passion, Renaissance foliage, profiles in medallions and putti blowing trumpets, all represented here. It is fascinating to reflect on the historical source of this material in Renaissance Italy, and the relative sophistication of the carving in this remote north Devon village. If only one could experience the congregation's exultation when they first beheld these bench ends in place.

The wagon roofs of the nave, chancel and west aisle, the arcade and sedilia are also attractive, but one regrets the stained- and frosted-glass windows which make an otherwise attractive interior gloomy.

HOLBETON
All Saints

9m/15km SE of Plymouth

The church is an impressive structure with a steeple and an especially roomy interior; dark, with two aisles. The screen, sensitively restored by J. D. Sedding in 1885-9, has on its north and south aisles original fifteenth-century wainscoting, but the rest is of fine craftsmanship, as are Sedding's benches and stalls with their oak-leaves and animals. In a chapel off the north aisle is an astonishing monument of three generations of Heles, with kneeling figures on four steps or tiers, and in their midst the semi-reclining figure of Sir Thomas Hele of Flete who died in 1624; a total of 23 people. Not to be missed. The more I encounter these Elizabethans the more I admire their vigour, self-confidence and incomparable sense of poetry.

HOLCOMBE BURNELL
St John the Baptist

4m/6km W of Exeter

A cosy, clear-lit country church of some charm. It stands alone surrounded by a landscape of wooded hills; no village but the early-seventeenth-century Barton (formerly the manor house) nearby. Originally of the twelfth century, the church was rebuilt by Hayward of Exeter in 1843-4 in fifteenth-century style. There is an arcade of four granite columns, wooden wagon roofs and several deep-set latticed windows, one of which, at the east end, contains fragments of mediaeval glass. This simple church with its neat pews has two outstanding features: an Easter Sepulchre which contains a large carving of the Resurrection, and a cut-down rood-screen with good (but dark) paintings of saints. The mottled stonework of the exterior is beautiful.

HOLCOMBE ROGUS
All Saints

8m/12km NE of Tiverton

Imagine a high wall running some 50 feet before you. On its left there is a gate through which a superb Tudor house set in a wooded landscape garden can be seen; on its right, a quiet lane leads to the church of All Saints, passing on the way a small Church (or Priest's) House. Nothing could be more appealing than this picturesque environment.

The interior is dominated by a rare example of a completely preserved Jacobean family pew (magnificent carving here), the Bluett pew. It encloses spectacular memorials to the family, who as owners of Holcombe Court were lay rectors for nearly 500 years. The earliest depicts Richard Bluett (d.1614) reclining on one elbow above the figure of his wife Mary (see page 222). The next commemorates Sir John Bluett (d.1634), dressed in armour, and his wife. They are recumbent, but their eight daughters kneel against the front of the tomb chest, facing east. Another Bluett, the Rev. Robert (d.1749), has a handsome alabaster memorial. A fine fifteenth-century wagon roof is enriched by a hundred foliage bosses.

HOLNE

St Mary the Virgin

4m/6km W of Ashburton

Built c.1300, this attractive church originally consisted of a central nave and chancel, with transepts and a western tower. Around 1500 the building was enlarged by the opening out of the transepts and addition of the side aisles with granite arcades. Today its mellow charm is characterised by the familiar features of so many other Devon church interiors – granite, stone, white walls, and dark tanned wood – to which here has been added the dazzling splendour of its elaborately carved and painted mediaeval screen. This dates from 1480-1500 and has been described by its restorer Anna Hulbert as "one of the most magnificent survivals of mediaeval colour and gilding in Devon". The cornice is sumptuously decorated with carvings of wheat and grapes (the bread and the wine of Communion), its wainscot panels, with recently restored paintings of 38 saints and martyrs. The pulpit, richly carved and of unusual design, on a goblet (not a

Screen and chancel bosses, St Mary the Virgin, Holne.

palm tree) foot, is of the same date as the screen.

The nave's wagon roofs are open, but those in the aisles are ceiled. The timeworn porch, with its granite entrance, paved floorway and stone seats, makes a charming entrance. There is an ancient yew tree in the churchyard.

HORWOOD

St Michael

3m/4km E of Bideford

As the guidebook observes, it is often impossible to know the exact age of an ancient building. This one, generally Perpendicular, is a case in point; the font and an eleventh-century piscina in the sanctuary are the sole survivors of the earliest building, Norman in date. The first definite mention of a church in Horwood comes in 1241.

The present one is a delightful little building, mostly c.1500. Apart from its nave and chancel it has a northern aisle (donated by a John Pollard in the early fifteenth century), and a meditative arcade of six Beer stone columns decorated with unusual capitals. The tower was added at the same time. The stairs to its top were unclimbable because of the depth of sticks left by the ravens building their nests. Displayed in the church is a bell frame made for the bell first pealed in 1664.

This simple country church is distinguished by several attractive features. They include four mediaeval stained-glass windows (in the lights of the east end window of the north chapel), a fine set of five bench ends with depictions of, amongst others, the symbols of Christ's Passion, several lead-glazed relief tiles, a Jacobean communion rail and an octagonal oak pulpit of the same period. There is also an important mid-fifteenth-century white alabaster monument of a recumbent lady

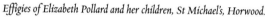
Effigies of Elizabeth Pollard and her children, St Michael's, Horwood.

with a sensitive face, possibly Elizabeth Pollard who died in 1430. She wears a horn-shaped headdress typical of the early fifteenth century and has, wrapped in the folds of her long mantle, four little children – another instance perhaps of the Madonna della Misericordia seen in early Italian painting. Tristram Risdon writing in 1630 observes the same sight as I do in 2007: "Elizabeth Pollard lies entombed, whose proportion in alabaster with two children on each side, is the most curiously cut as any I have seen."

The slate and stone of the aisle floor are worn smooth by the footsteps of countless worshippers. The sunshine, filtering through the clear-glass window panes, washes it with a devotional light. What beauty! Outside, the sound of bird music adds to the enchantment.

IPPLEPEN
St Andrew

3m/4km SW of Newton Abbot
St Andrew's is a large church, almost entirely of the fifteenth century and immaculately maintained. It has a noble west tower, about 85 feet high (unfortunately rendered with grey cement), a nave and two aisles. The interior is well proportioned and possesses

two notable features: a handsome but restored rood-screen with a cornice embellished with carving of leaves, grapes and birds, and a gorgeous fifteenth-century pulpit – gold, green, vermilion – approached by a charming eighteenth-century stair. There is also a Georgian brass chandelier and a much worn but fascinating Norman tympanum above a narrow north door.

In the evening when the sun is shining, the silhouetted chandelier, seen against the clear-glassed Perpendicular windows, is most beautiful.

KELLY
St Mary the Virgin

5m/8km SE of Launceston
Passing through a scattered village enveloped in the heat of an early summer afternoon (the sound of a lawnmower the one indication of habitation), one reaches Kelly church, in the usual fifteenth-century style with a tower, five-bay arcade of granite piers and an extensively restored late mediaeval window. Rather dull interior, but comely. The graveyard is luxuriantly spotted with the flowers of lady's smocks and dandelion heads amongst the grass.

KENTISBEARE

St Mary

3m/4km E of Cullompton

St Mary's in the Blackdown hills has an exceptionally handsome tower. The buttresses and stair turret of a chequer pattern of blocks of white Beer stone alternate with a rare cinnamon-brown variety of the new red sandstone from a quarry at Upton. This design is unique in Devon. Four figures representing the beasts of the Apocalypse are set at each angle below the battlements. The same stone, but of a pinkier hue, is on the north side of the church, facing the approaching visitor. The tracery of its Perpendicular windows is especially sensitive.

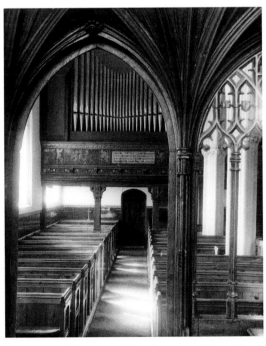

The north aisle looking towards the gallery, St Mary's, Kentisbeare.

The interior is largish, filled with remarkable objects, but to my taste somewhat over-upholstered (another red carpet does not help here). Its early sixteenth-century south aisle, divided from the nave by four Beer stone columns with carved capitals (one of a woolsack and a ship), is lit by a sequence of generously sized Perpendicular windows. This aisle, as wide and spacious as the nave, contains a small chapel built in memory of a Tudor merchant venturer called John Whiting (d.1529), who gave his money for the building of the aisle. A carved table tomb to his memory, and that of his wife Anne is in this chapel.

The ten-bay screen is the church's most luxuriant feature, and one of the finest in the county. The carving of the cornice, composed of four bands of grapes and vines, is richly detailed, its ancient colouring, red and gold in places, is handsome.

Another attractive feature is the hefty wooden gallery dating from 1632, which extends across the western end of the church. It has painted panels and twelve lines of verse ending with the couplet: "The reason why these lines are set to view/ It is because the poor should have their due."

Most of the windows are of clear glass except for the one in the chancel by Clayton and Bell, 1882. This is a full-blooded Victorian space with a heavy-handed but gutsy marble and mosaic reredos. The pine pews, which date from the restoration of 1865-6, are unattractive.

On the east side of the churchyard is an ancient yew tree, supposedly a thousand years old.

KENTON

All Saints

4m/6km N of Dawlish

This is a large, late fourteenth-century building in a handsome setting. Its churchyard bursting with tombstones is lined by modest eighteenth- and nineteenth-century houses. The church, built of a deep red conglomerate with shards of darker rock fused into the stone, has an especially fine exterior; a splendid tower and a wonderful porch, which possesses a charming and richly decorated niche from which its original figure is missing. The two entrances consist of a square-headed outer and inner porch

Monk on the screen at Kenton.

doorway, both carved in Beer stone. On the occasion of my visit, a swallow was flying backwards and forwards attending to its young in the porch.

The interior is spacious, light-filled and majestically calm, but like other Perpendicular churches, is not atmospheric. The piers which process on either side of the nave with a serene but unexciting dignity are of Beer stone, the pews are sternly Victorian, the reredos is dull. The chief attraction is the massive screen and ten-foot rood-loft – restored over a number of years by the ubiquitous Herbert Read (see pages 200 and 201). The carving may be slightly academic, but the wainscoting is decorated with 40 painted panels of saints and prophets dating from 1455. The fifteenth-century pulpit was much restored in 1882 from pieces rescued by Baring-Gould.

LANDCROSS
Holy Trinity

3m/5km S of Bideford
A small, hidden-away church in a small graveyard in what is reputed to be the smallest parish in Devon. It is built of stone in

the Perpendicular style, with an unaffected whitewashed chancel, a nave with a ceiled wagon roof, and a south porch. It has a projecting slate-hung wall turret (containing just one bell) which replaced a tower destroyed by lightning c.1820. The only remaining feature suggesting an earlier church on this site is the font of later Norman style, with a cushion-shaped bowl of grey stone. There are some sixteenth-century bench ends, a very dark Royal Arms of King George II dated 1731, and an attractive tiled floor. But simplicity is the keynote here; the mood is one of much loved rural simplicity.

LANDKEY
St Paul

1m/2km E of Barnstaple
This country church lies beyond the depressingly suburbanised village of Landkey and close to open fields. Perpendicular and strangely unfocussed, the interior nonetheless contains charming features such as a fine painted roof, a lovely west window in the north aisle, a painted Minstrels' Gallery, and a sensitively carved early fourteenth-century monument of a cross-legged knight and his lady wearing a wimple. Her feet are resting on a dog. Also remarkable is the large standing wall monument to Sir Arthur Acland (d.1610) and his wife, crudely painted in a naive pasteboard style but enchanting nonetheless. Both figures, inadvertently amusing, are recumbent, and with a falcon that resembles a parrot.

LAPFORD
St Thomas of Canterbury

5m/8km SE of Chulmleigh
Although this fifteenth-century church has an unattractive interior – scraped, potato-coloured walls, a gloomy light, an ugly Victorian pulpit and an unimpressive chancel – it is a scene of some of the finest

Facing page: The cornice of the screen at St Thomas of Canterbury, Lapford.

furnishings in the county. The chief of these is the exceptionally fine rood-screen (probably constructed in the second quarter of the sixteenth century) which is about 32 feet long and carved on both sides. It has much delicately carved Renaissance detail between the vaulting ribs, and a complete cornice. Here the fruits swell and burgeon with enormous vitality, and a flowing vine motif (alluding to Christ the True Vine and to the wine of the Eucharist) twines its way along its length.

There is a large array of bench ends (c.1530-40), a short parclose screen, and a nave roof with angel corbels at the foot of each principal. The wooden celure above the screen is superb.

LEW TRENCHARD
St Peter

8m/12km E of Launceston

On the day of my visit, the path to the church was resplendent with a wide verge of bluebells and daisies. I chatted with an old man scything the churchyard grass, and our topic of discussion centred on the Rev. Sabine Baring-Gould (1834-1924), one of Devon's most talented and celebrated parsons, who was rector here for 43 years. "I

The Breton eagle lectern at Lew Trenchard.

felt I had a work to do, not like that of Newman in England at large, but at Lewtrenchard the small . . ."

Theologian, antiquarian, novelist, hymn writer and reformer, Baring-Gould collected the folk-songs of Devon and wrote over a hundred books. He was also the Squire and Rector of Lew Trenchard, and from the date of his induction he set about undoing the damage which had been perpetrated by his grandfather, who had removed the mediaeval rood-screen. Baring-Gould had already salvaged the fragments as a boy, and set about the screen's reconstruction at the end of the century. This work also contains painted panels and a loft which, I felt, dominated this smallish church, which includes furniture – a pulpit (modelled on those in the churches of Kenton and Launceston) and bench ends, clergy stalls, a chandelier and a lectern – which Baring-Gould had purchased from somewhere else, often the Continent. Does this assemblage fully succeed? Although John Betjeman describes the interior as "almost overwhelming in its beauty", I do not think this is so. It is attractive, but feels artificial, although the wooden sixteenth-century lectern from Brittany in the form of a beady-eyed golden eagle is very fine. There is also a rare cast-iron stove still in place, occasionally used to keep the church warm.

LITTLEHAM
St Swithun

3m/5km S of Bideford

Bucketfuls of rain overnight, but today the world washed and shining as if new-made; lesser celandines glinting in the tall churchyard grass and daffodils and primroses in flower in the hedgerows. It is only the first week in March, yet it could be April already. The setting, wooded and elevated, remote from the village, is one of undisturbed serenity.

The interior is also pervaded by peace. It has a wondrous rood-screen designed by

Temple Moore, apparently based on that of Partrishow in Monmouthshire. It is finely carved, courtly, golden. No less remarkable are the fine stained-glass windows by the Kempe studios, and the substantial tomb with an alabaster effigy of General Greacock (1891), also by Temple Moore. These were features introduced by Rev. G. Morse who instigated the restoration in 1892.

There is an early fourteenth-century painting of Christ of the Trades, with scales, an ancient muniment chest, a decorated sage-green panelled barrel vault, and a considerable number of bench ends with early Renaissance features. Nonetheless, these features, alongside the shining screen, the heavy Victorian tomb and ornamental wooden vault, make for an harmonious if unexpected ensemble.

LUFFINCOTT
St James

The church is discovered in remote countryside a few miles beyond Tetcott and even closer to the Cornish border. Architecturally it may have little significance, but its humility is arresting. So too is its

Luppitt: the roof crossing and Green Man.

Luppitt: detail of the font.

setting. With no village (the parish has a population of 45), it stands almost in the farmyard of Luffincott Barton; to get to it one crosses a field. As Alec Clifton-Taylor has observed, "Some of the loveliest churches are the loneliest. All over England one finds them, often beautifully sited, with no habitation in sight, and many more with only a single house, although often a big one. These are amongst the least spoiled of our churches."

St James is one of these. Though predominantly of the fifteenth century, it has a squattish limewashed west tower with obelisk pinnacles built in 1791 and on the north side of its nave sash windows of the eighteenth century. The interior is extremely simple (nave and chancel united) and deeply rustic, but with one exceptional feature: attractively carved bosses on its boarded wagon roof.

It is in the care of the Churches Conservation Trust.

LUPPITT
St Mary

Approached by way of steep, undulating lanes with views of the valley of the Otter beneath, the isolated village of Luppitt (population 444) stands on a hillside at c.500 feet.

Its church, largely of the fourteenth century (but restored in the late 1880s), is of no particular architectural distinction, apart from its famous Norman font (see page 214) and equally spectacular wagon roof. The font is deeply and vigorously carved with a barbaric confidence which may have a special appeal for our emasculated age. On one side there are representations of the martyrdom of an early Christian by the local pagan chieftain (see page 215); on another, a carving of an Amphisbaena, a double-headed monster representing the evils of duplicity; and on a third, possibly a representation of the Tree of Life – a pattern of enfolded organic interlacings. Observe how the stone head in the south-west corner of the font has been worn down by generations of priests bending over to christen the infant in their arms. Tucked away in a corner of the chancel, and easily missed, is another vigorous piece of carving, a rare Norman pillar piscina. It is worth seeking out.

The late mediaeval wagon roofs over the nave and transepts, a dark umber colour, are an unselfconscious celebration of the mediaeval synthesis of beauty and utility. The timbers meeting at the crossing with a boss of a Green Man are reminiscent of the hold of a mighty mediaeval ship. The energy, the power of this roof, are worth travelling a considerable distance to see.

MANATON
St Winifred

3m/4km S of Moretonhampstead

A delightful granite church with a limewashed tower in a wonderful setting high in the eastern foothills of Dartmoor: nearby is a green lined with lime trees. Opposite it, beyond the gravestones, there is the village cricket field, with a pavilion and nets, and rising behind that a moorland hillside.

Mostly rebuilt in the fifteenth century, but renovated by Herbert Read c.1945, St Winifred's has a wonderful interior. There is an exceptionally fine eleven-bay rood-screen,

Cornice of the rood-screen, St Winifred, Manaton.

extending across the nave and both aisles, and a screen with two decorated cornice bands, a wainscot with painted saints, and small statuettes in the jambs and voussoirs. There is some original colour and gilding.

There is also an Easter Sepulchre, but in the chancel some unfortunate stained-glass windows, including one based on a design by Frank Brangwyn. The silence is remarkable.

In the churchyard there are ancient headstones dating from the late sixteenth century onwards.

MARYSTOW
St Mary the Virgin

6m/10km NW of Tavistock

Another forgotten church in the country west of Dartmoor, whose spirit colours its atmosphere, stands by itself on a sloping hillside. The external appearance is especially delightful, with a series of differing window designs and a tower about 50 feet high, diagonally buttressed on all corners. The interior is also attractive, but not inspiring. There is a six-bay granite arcade, a series of clear-glass latticed windows, some wagon roofs, a double-headed fourteenth-century sedilia and a Norman font large enough for infant immersion. Regrettably, the walls have been scraped, the pulpit insensitively carved, and the Victorian tiles around the altar are of a repellent design.

The church houses one of the most ambitious monuments in Devonshire: the ostentatiously large Renaissance tomb for Sir Thomas Wyse (1629) and his wife. Dame Margery's slippered feet peep out of the folds of her voluminous dress.

MONKLEIGH
St George

3m/4km NW of Torrington

We set off for Monkleigh on a ripe, lustrous afternoon, the trees browning, the hedgerows shaven, the fields alive with

Pelican on the screen at Monkleigh.

scurrying pheasants; it is early October, and the fullness of the season is at its richest.

The tower of the church is a landmark for miles, standing sentinel on its hilltop; it is a feature of the wooded Torridge valley. It had a mighty presence against a dark cobalt sky. The interior shares much the same bare, elevated feeling; all granite, dark oak, slate and sparkling light.

Perhaps its greatest attraction is its south aisle, the Annery aisle, named after Sir William Hankford of Annery who left money for its completion and maintenance on condition that he and his heirs should have a burial place therein. That was in 1423. The aisle and its large Perpendicular windows remain striking. Hankford's canopied altar-tomb is a delight, and so are the brilliant tangerine-orange panes of Renaissance glass in the windows. At the time of our visit these glowed in the afternoon sun with a fiery splendour.

Although the church contains many beautiful and fascinating features – a sturdy sixteenth-century screen, some well-carved bench ends, a number of mediaeval tiles, an unusually designed Norman font, two sensitively engraved slate monuments (1627 and 1646) and a melancholy monument to William Gaye (d.1631) and his wife – it is the Annery chapel which compels the most attention. But also note the lock box of the south door, carved with a monster, and the charming cobbles set on the floor of the south porch. In the graveyard there are several well-lettered seventeenth- and eighteenth-century slate tombstones. The views of the surrounding countryside are superb.

MORCHARD BISHOP
St Mary

6m/10km NW of Crediton
The church surmounts an upland village once situated on the old turnpike road from Crediton to Barnstaple, but re-routed in the 1820s. Its west tower continues to dominate the village and much of the surrounding countryside.

St Mary's is another almost off-the-peg Perpendicular building, whose design was hardly enhanced by the restoration of 1887-91. At this time, its walls were scraped and an

Bench ends, St Mary the Virgin, Mortehoe.

insensitive tiled floor and dado installed. Nonetheless the church contains some features of great charm, particularly the panelled, white-painted, eighteenth-century chancel and the elaborate rood-screen. This was another achievement of the ubiquitous Herbert Read, between 1928 and 1940. The two recumbent figures are supposed to be of a Devonshire franklin and his wife dating from the early sixteenth century.

On the day of our visit the church was decorated with beautiful Easter flowers – white daisies and lilies – and a charming mossy Easter Sepulchre.

MORELEIGH
All Saints

3m/4km S of Totnes
An enchanting little early fourteenth-century church, lovely in itself and filled with attractive features. The most dominant is the stately, stiff-necked pulpit with a tester like an eighteenth-century hat. There is also a delicious fawn and golden Queen Anne Coat of Arms, a dumpy Norman font and a readers' desk reconstituted from parts of the original screen. The chancel roof was simply patterned in the seventeenth century when the church was restored. More recently someone with a delightful sense of colour has decorated the simple splendour of this charming interior.

MORTEHOE
St Mary the Virgin

4m/6km W of Ilfracombe
Architecturally, St Mary's may not be exceptional, but it is special nonetheless – partly on account of its isolated position close to the striking cliff scenery of the north Devon coast, partly because of the Morte Slate out of which it has been partially constructed, and partly because of its comfortable human scale.

It dates from around 1170, when William de Tracey, one of the knights who murdered Thomas à Becket, is supposed to have founded the church as part of his penance. In the thirteenth century it was enlarged with a chancel and perhaps a south transept. Even with its Perpendicular north transept added, it remains a small community church.

The interior has a sombre strength and is simple and unfussed. It is the place where generations of Mortehoe men and women met to worship, to mourn their dead, to signal births and marriages and celebrate important events in local and national life. It was their church, as it was their predecessors', and would be their children's too.

An unexpected feature is the large mosaic of a Byzantine pre-Raphaelite character on the chancel arch. It was designed by Selwyn Image, Slade Professor of Art at Oxford in 1903, and executed by the craftsmen who made the mosaics in St Paul's Cathedral. Image also contributed the four stained glass panels of angels in the diagonal transept windows. Not perhaps exceptional, but atmospheric in an attractive way.

The church has 48 bench ends and a large tomb chest in the south transept, probably to the Reverend William de Tracey, rector of Mortehoe (d.1322), but of uncertain attribution.

NEWTON ABBOT
St Mary, Abbotsbury

Waverley Road

Outside, its proportions are deceptive. It sits long and low and rhythmically buttressed, halfway up a hill in the centre of Newton Abbot, amongst terraces of houses. Inside, it feels long and high, a generous but friendly space, enveloped by the sweeping barrel roof, and divided only by narrow passage aisles. You cannot fully feel its length, for the two west bays have been screened off, to the height of the arches, to create offices. It is by

the Arts and Crafts architect E. H. Sedding, and unlike his earlier mysterious interior at Shaldon, it is light and airy, helped by the great west window with its swirling tracery (Pevsner calls it "wild"), and by the beautiful pale stone of its walls. The wooden fittings are rewarding: the massive open screen, which unlike mediaeval Devon screens stretches upwards rather than across, and only resembles its ancestors when it reaches the two elaborate bands of cornice; the high bulky pulpit complete with tester; the choir stalls, the parclose screen, the altar frontal and the reredos, with its scene of the shepherds worshipping at the manger. All are richly carved: squirrels in the cornice, corn on the communion rail (made of marble), even a little angel band of musicians on the legs of the pulpit. The east window is fifteenth century, culled from Highweek Chapel, and decorated on the inside by family badges. When I had arranged to collect the key, the churchwarden, Mr Tapley, warned me to expect a spectacular interior. I was not disappointed.

"Wild tracery" in west window, St Mary's, Abbotsbury.

NEWTON ST CYRES

St Cyres & St Julitta

3m/4km SE of Crediton

Snowdrops were in flower along the hedge banks and lambs were grazing in the fields on our way to the village. Entering the church of St Cyres and St Julitta (a Roman lady and her four-year old son, martyred for defying Diocletian's edict that banned Christian worship), I was temporarily blinded by the impact of great blades of fiery light and the airy beauty of the interior. Branches of flowering hazels were spread around the church.

It is a warm-hearted place, beautifully maintained and filled with treasures: a fine Beer-stone arcade, a handsome mahogany canopied pulpit; a Flemish carved panel of Christ turning water into wine attached to the lectern (see page 218); old wagon roofs; and its *pièce de résistance*, a monument to John Northcote of Hayne of 1632. He is a haunting full-sized figure of a soldier, dressed in full armour, with high boots, a sword and baton, reminiscent of the Commendatore in Mozart's *Don Giovanni*. To

One of John Northcote's wives kneeling at his feet.

Detail of Northcote monument, Newton St Cyres.

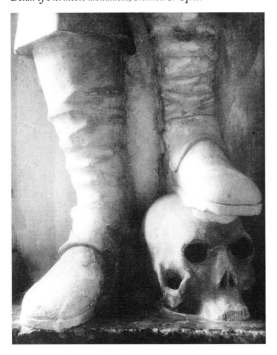

the left and right of this figure are the busts of his two wives with the following intriguing inscriptions: the first reads, "My fruite was small/ One Sonne was all/ That not at all". And the second: 'My Jacob had by mee/ as many sons as hee/ Daughters twice three." Below the standing figure of Northcote are those of his son, wife and children (original colouring) and two babies placed on the ground.

The church contains a rare King James II arms, and further monuments dating back to the seventeenth century. These are of the Quicke family, still resident in the village and making excellent cheese.

NORTH BOVEY

St John the Baptist

2m/3km SW of Moretonhampstead

Approached along narrow, winding, high-hedged lanes stuffed with bracken, North Bovey (population 274) is situated on Dartmoor's eastern fringe. Village and parish had at one time a larger population than today, yet despite the changes which have

Mediaeval benches, St John the Baptist, North Bovey.

taken place over the years, descendants of the old yeoman families – such as Windeat and Crout, whose granite memorials are in the church – still flourish in the area,

Although each is subtly different, the church at North Bovey has much in common with those of Throwleigh and Manaton. It consists of a nave, supported by monolithic octagonal granite piers with open aisles to north and south. East of this lies the chancel, the sanctuary, the Lady Chapel and a space now in use as a vestry for both priest and server. There is an attractive fifteenth-century carved screen stretching across the nave and aisles (its coving missing), many old bench ends and, above the sanctuary which retains its ceiled wagon roof, a series of good bosses with subjects similar to those at Widecombe. One of these depicts three rabbits with ears conjoined in a triangle – an emblem also found in other churches on, or not far from, Dartmoor. There is a simple flagstone floor, blessedly without a red carpet.

The fabric, with its attractive concord of stone and wood, is lovingly maintained. I admired an exquisite vase of violet and purple flowers and the sombre but light-filled quality of the interior – dark umber, white, grey.

NORTH HUISH
St Mary

8m/12km SW of Totnes

A silent place, bare but characterful. Overlooking a hilly wooded valley, the church with a stone spire and slate hung tower is cared for by the Churches Conservation Trust. Its interior is attractively proportioned, simple and unostentatious. It has slate floors,

The monument to Amyas Bamfylde and his family, All Saints, North Molton.

sinewy wagon roofs and except for a crucifixion in the east window, it is without stained glass. There is an ornate mediaeval rood-screen in the south aisle and a font of 1662. To greet the visitor there were bunches of deep cobalt hydrangea flowers on either side of the entrance porch.

NORTH MOLTON
All Saints

3m/4km NE of South Molton
The largely late fourteenth-century church towers above this isolated township, once prosperous with its own woollen and mining industries, still charming but now industrially inactive. In front of the church and its proud and stately three-stage tower,

there is an open space and a graveyard.

All Saints has an attractive interior, spacious, light-filled and welcoming. On the day of my visit it was decorated with many flowers, lilies and daffodils. On top of the font were six pots of pristine primroses.

There is an elegant nave with a five-bay arcade and, unusually, a clerestory. It has some lovely wagon roofs with bosses and plastered panels, a fine Perpendicular rood-screen, octagonal font, and wooden pulpit of 1700 with a trumpeting angel on the tester. More unusual is its most striking feature, the dark brown chancel panelling brought from Court House in the 1840s, richly carved with heads, stags and heraldic lions.

Of great charm, too, is the large standing alabaster wall-monument which features Sir

Amyas Bamfylde (d.1626) with his wife seated at his feet and their seventeen children kneeling in a frozen kind of way, as for a group photograph. It has retained its original railings.

From North Molton we made our way across the spectacular countryside of wooded combes and naked, steep-sided hills, to the upland village of Molland. All the way the grass glowed with the luminous bosses of flowering primroses, and was busy with sheep and their ever-gambolling lambs.

NYMET ROWLAND
St Bartholomew

4m/6km S of Chulmleigh

The church of this attractively named village has an unsophisticated pastoral interior, a Norman south door and font, four sixteenth-century oak benches and a splendid Royal Coat of Arms (1792) bearing the names of two people whose families are still common in the district, the churchwarden J. Partridge and the painter, Passmore.

Regrettably, the pitch pine pews and the chancel, restored in 1874, strike a meaner note than the generous proportions of the celebrated wooden arcade which divides the nave from the north aisle.

On our visit we met Victoria Littlewood, churchwarden, and, it seems, the church's guardian angel. Such optimism and commitment will be important for the survival of this and other parish churches.

OFFWELL
St Mary

2m/3km E of Honiton

On the day of my visit – a grey January morning – the interior of this bare but pleasing church had an atmosphere of breathless stillness. There were bare flagged floors and a luminous north aisle whose windows were flooding the church with light.

In contrast, the chancel was rather dark, but on its south side there was a small window glowing with mediaeval glass – royal blues, maroon-red and orange – all jumbled up. There were also box pews, a Georgian pulpit with carved figures of the evangelists and a reader's desk. At the western end of the nave, the tower screen was filled with two bays from a richly coloured mediaeval screen brought here from St Mary Major in Exeter in 1870.

In the churchyard are several yews, the oldest probably planted about 1650, another in 1804.

PAIGNTON
St John the Baptist

3m/4km SW of Torquay

The town of Paignton, located in the central area of Torbay, has an ancient church set in an oasis of trees, but one surrounded by buildings worn ugly with seaside commerce. On the occasion of our visit, the contrast favoured the heavenly calm of the church, its powerful red sandstone building set against an enamelled June sky

Paignton was an ancient village. The early settlement was half a mile inland, while marshes bordered the sea. St John's stands on a Saxon settlement and incorporates some Norman work such as the north and south rubble walls of the chancel, the red font, and the west door with its dog-tooth decoration. There have been, in fact, not two but three or even four churches on the site. The third dates from the fourteenth century, when the north and south aisles, the doorways, south porch and lower half of the tower were built. About 1450-1500 it was again largely rebuilt in red sandstone, when the aisles were heightened, the transepts and the two choir chapels erected, and the tower completed. At the Reformation, the Reformers called a stop to further development and damaged much that had been built. Subsequent years

have seen the restoration of the church to something approaching its earlier appearance.

All this was unknown to me when I entered the building and was faced by a delightful and warm-hearted interior; faced, too, by a small army of industrious cleaners who greeted us with obvious pleasure. A few churches are locked; others encourage visitors. This one (open at set times) made us feel especially welcome.

The stone screen of the Kirkham Chantry (c.1490-1500), although vandalised by Puritans, is the chief interest of the interior. It consists of two Tudor-arched openings with tall tombstones and an entrance. Every surface of this remarkable structure has been ornately enriched with statues and reliefs. It was erected by the Kirkhams of Blagdon, and includes the recumbent figures of (probably) Nicholas Kirkham (1434-1516) and the nine orders of angels, four doctors of the church, four evangelists, the twelve apostles, as well as mourners in contemporary clothes. The chantry also includes a charming monument of two kneeling figures, one facing the other.

There is an early Norman font – the earliest in Devon – and an especially lovely Norman sandstone pulpit.

PILTON
St Mary

1m/2km or so N from the centre of Barnstaple
Approached through an archway, on cobbled paths and alongside a row of delightful 'Tudor' almshouses (1849), St Mary's enjoys a setting of exceptional charm, almost secret and most certainly not of this century. In its day, Pilton was more prosperous and important than Barnstaple, but those positions have been reversed. The church, originally part of a Benedictine priory founded in the twelfth century, is now a quiet and countrified kind of place.

Its interior is spacious, sombre in feeling, even noble, with a nave about as wide as it is long. The north aisle is separated from it by three massive unadorned arches; the south aisle by a slender Perpendicular arcade. There are wagon roofs to each, but that of the chancel is open-timbered. On the church's southernmost wall there are some large windows, all but one filled with lugubrious Victorian glass. The rigidly set pine pews are no less unappealing.

Yet in spite of this, the church is characterised by a noble simplicity, and contains several attractive features. Across the nave and south aisle there is a rich rood-screen (enhanced by ancient painting of saints on its wainscot panels); there is a handsome pulpit with an outstretched iron hand holding an hour-glass to control the length of the sermon and with recycled Renaissance carved panels, a Tudor cover and a projecting tester. Another (late Perpendicular) stone pulpit has a crisply shaped sounding board. There are also three fine monuments – the handsomest is dated 1627, consisting of the life-sized kneeling figures of Sir Robert Chichester, his two wives, a daughter and the couple's two younger children. The other monument, figureless but busy with well-carved strap-work cartouches, was erected in 1569, to another Chichester. On the south wall, clumsily placed between two windows, is a large and vigorous wall monument to Christopher Lethbridge of 1713, The Elizabethan altar table and the large painted Royal Arms of Queen Anne (1707) are also attractive.

PLYMOUTH
St Andrew

Catherine Street
Although St Andrew's is externally dull, even coarse, its extensive interior provides an exhilarating experience. On the occasion of my visit, its grey, magnanimous civic

architecture was flooded with powerful mid-September light which glowed victoriously through its large plain nave windows, and more especially its eastern stained-glass ones. Dating from 1958, these were designed by the painter John Piper (1903-1992) and made by his collaborator Patrick Reyntiens. It is unusual to find something as radiantly imaginative belonging to the twentieth century.

There are in all six windows: one in the tower portraying the incidents surrounding the crucifixion of Jesus (blues, green and flashes of red), three at the east end displaying the emblems of the Virgin Mary (deep blues, yellows, reds and white), the four elements of creation – water, earth, fire and air – (green, red and white) and a window with the wheel of St Catherine (hot reds and pinks). Other windows celebrate the powers of inspiration and music (amber and yellow) and in the south transept, the Creation and the Trinity (blues, whites and greens). Piper's contribution lifts the heart.

Looking at his work took me back to some words of the architect Sir Ninian Comper from an article of 1939, 'Of the Atmosphere of a Church': "The atmosphere of a church should be such as to hush the thoughtless voice. . . . The purpose of a church is not to express the age in which it was built or the individuality of its designer. Its purpose is to move to worship, to bring a man to his knees, to refresh his soul in a weary land. This is the Creator's purpose towards Man in giving him the beauty of Nature, and it should be the purpose of all art."

A display in the tower shows photographs of the burnt-out church, much of which (including the Victorian glass) was destroyed by incendiary bombs during the night of 22nd March 1941. Fortunately the stonework survived, and the church has been excellently restored and given new roofs (1949-57).

PLYMPTON ST MARY
St Mary the Blessed Virgin

4m/6km E from Plymouth centre

Built by the canons of Plympton Priory, this largely early fifteenth-century church stands alone in a large graveyard surrounded by the unprepossessing environment of outer Plymouth. Characterised by civic pride, the building has a wide nave and a double set of aisles. It is grand, but confusing and perhaps a trifle boring. There is, however, at least one redeeming feature: a small but exquisite vaulted roof to its south porch (c.1400). There are also two attractive monuments: one dated 1637 with the busts of ten children, another a tomb chest, to Sir Richard Strode of 1464.

RATTERY
St Mary

5m/8km W of Totnes

The church preserves its early cruciform plan of the thirteenth century, but was remodelled in the fifteenth when the transepts were enlarged into aisles. The interior is dark, even gloomy, but moodily atmospheric. The font is Norman. The nine-bay screen dates from the fifteenth century. The interior walls are decorated with an unusual sgraffito scheme of c.1870.

The tower is unusually tapering and has a steeple. The Church House, now an inn, is adjacent to the churchyard.

REVELSTOKE
St Peter the Poor Fisherman

Noss Mayo, 3m/4km SW of Yealmpton

Dramatically situated, this rugged ruin of a church is approached down the steepish path of a wooded cliffside overlooking a caravan site and the silvery waters of Stoke Bay. It has,

the Churches Conservation leaflet observes, a strangely monastic air. Abandoned around 1870 in favour of a new church, the old mediaeval building is largely roofless and denuded of tombs, glass, piers and pews. Yet its chancel has a strangely compelling atmosphere, romantic, poignant and sad.

RINGMORE
All Hallows

5m/10km E of Kingsbridge

It is the painting you come to see in this small church, built about 1240. When a nineteenth-century incumbent, the Rev. F. C. Hingeston, removed the plaster from above the chancel arch with his own hands, he uncovered remarkable decoration, which looks like mediaeval wallpaper supplied by Liberty's, a repeated pattern of a stylised plant form in red, green and black. Just beyond the chancel arch is the organ, whose pipes were most prettily painted in the 1860s (see page 15). The little screen is also nicely painted. The aisleless nave, however, suffers from the most unfortunate rendering, and you wish that somebody would paint that too – even white would help.

Mediaeval wall painting, All Hallows, Ringmore.

The church, perched above the village, has a battlemented tower like a toy fort, with the shortest of spires. In the churchyard is an ancient leaning yew (see page 211).

SALCOMBE REGIS
St Mary and St Peter

2m/3km NE of Sidmouth

Salcombe Regis is an idyllic place. On the afternoon of our visit the village was mounting, in and around the church, a summer fête. The place and the event reminded me of the articles that used to appear in *Picture Post* in the early years of the Second World War, articles reminding its readers what the country was fighting to preserve: England idealised.

Small but homely, the church was decorated with flowers, one arrangement in the font, a sprouting of ferns, foxgloves and alstroemerias, like a green fountain of leaves.

Originally twelfth century, the building is now a mixture of different styles and periods. About 1300 its chancel was lengthened, a south aisle added, and the arches of the north arcade remodelled, leaving the Norman pillars intact. Then in the 1430s further improvements were considered: the aisles were widened and provided with new windows.

An enlightened act of patronage: the recently installed reredos created by the glass engraver, Lawrence Whistler, and finished by his son, Simon, after his father's death. Its subject is the redemption of Creation through the Cross of Jesus Christ.

SANDFORD
St Swithin

2m/3km NW of Crediton

Set in the midst of an exceptionally delightful village and adjacent to a handsome fronted Congregational chapel, the parish church of Sandford has a somewhat

St Mary the Virgin, Silverton.

unprepossessing exterior. Its interior however is surprisingly large and neat, with many highly polished bench ends and a memorial screen designed by Caröe (1921-2). The church has a Jacobean west gallery (1657) with an elaborately carved front and the grand, if not grandiloquent, memorial to Sir John Davie of nearby Creedy Park (1692). In spite of its secular atmosphere, I admired the uninhibited vitality of this monument.

SILVERTON
St Mary the Virgin

4m/6km SW of Cullompton

White and airy and glowing with light, St Mary's spacious interior is an unexpected delight. It dates from about 1450 onwards and although typically Perpendicular has a charming individuality of its own. There are large windows (all but three of which are clear glass), a north parclose screen, a four-arch arcade, angel capitals, a wagon roof and a west gallery (of 1734) with bulbous wooden fluted pillars. Its nineteenth-century brass light fittings are also worthy of attention.

On leaving the church, note the cobbled path and by the south porch a massive yew tree. There is also a grove of stately limes, said to have been planted to commemorate the restoration of the monarchy in 1660. On the day of our visit – it was the first day of November – their shivering golden leaves glowed in the low, raking autumn sunlight.

SOUTH BRENT

St Petroc

5m/8km SW of Buckfastleigh

The first thing that strikes you on entering is the splendid red sandstone circular Norman font with its cable, palmette and zigzag decoration. After that, much of the rest of the church comes as a disappointment: the energy is weaker, there is less conviction. Originally, St Petroc's was a small cruciform Norman building of which only the massive crossing tower (today the west tower) survives. By 1246 the nave had been rebuilt and two further bays (now the north and south aisles) were added. Further developments included the north and south transepts and chancel in the fifteenth century. In 1870 the church was restored, its walls scraped, the rood-screen removed and the present pulpit introduced. Today the atmosphere, if roomy, is a bit impersonal and even oppressive. An especially unattractive feature is the insensitive pointing of the pillars in dark grey mortar. But the old south porch door is magnificent.

SOUTH POOL

St Nicholas and St Cyriacus

3m/4km S of Kingsbridge

Approached in the pouring rain, the great slate-built tower and fifteenth century church were both black and glistening – the latter moodily dark inside. Nonetheless, there was enough light to see and admire its astonishing pale honey-coloured rood-screen whose carving, firm and handsome, must be some of Devon's most accomplished. It has

Rood-screen, St Nicholas and St Cyriacus, South Pool.

Base of tower, St Andrew's, South Tawton.

three cornice friezes and a series of ghostly paintings in the wainscot,

Of lesser beauty is the Easter Sepulchre in the north chancel wall, now occupied by the tomb and effigy of Thomas Bryan who was rector here in 1536. In the south aisle there is a wall monument to Leonard Darre, his wife and five children, dating from 1608.

SOUTH TAWTON
St Andrew

4m/6km E of Okehampton

On the day of our visit, great baroque clouds rose against the deep blue sky behind the 75-foot tower. It is of granite ashlar, with impressive buttresses, and has tall, slim pinnacles shaped like obelisks, which give it elegance.

Opening the door into the church (always a moment of excitement), one is astonished by its scale, its handsome furnishings and atmosphere of light-filled elegance. The Beer stone arches of the nave are beautiful; there is a fine dark-brown wagon roof and an astonishing screen with lace-like tracery. It dates from 1902 and is a remarkable addition. The same can also be said of the Victorian glass (some by Clayton and Bell), such as the window in the north aisle. However, most are clear-glassed, which gives this interior its clarity. It is most beautifully lit.

Besides some elegant altar-rails with twisty balusters, the church has an exquisite eighteenth-century pulpit inlaid with figures of the Evangelists (see page 218), and two attractive monuments. That of John Weekes in the north chapel dates from 1572. The captain is seen lying beneath a low tester, his feet resting, for some strange reason, on a duck. The other, more naive but especially tender, is in the south-east corner of the Lady Chapel. It is in the form of a slate, onto which have been etched the figures of six kneeling sons, two kneeling daughters and two infants, one in swaddling clothes. Above these, their parents, Robert Burgoyne and his wife, are represented in effigy. The date is 1651.

The layout of the churchyard, the winding village street, the early twentieth-century lychgate and unspoilt early sixteenth-century Church House, are a magnificent example of unintentional village planning.

SOWTON
St Michael

Outskirts of Exeter, near the A30

Sowton is not just a roundabout and a business park. Far away from these, but near the A30, is the old village of cob and thatch houses which feels as though it belongs to a remote part of rural Devon. And sure enough, down a long lane, there is a red sandstone mediaeval church. But all is not as it appears. The lovely north arcade of angel capitals is the first impression of the interior, and this is fifteenth-century (see pages 208 and 209). The rest is by John Hayward, who rebuilt it in 1845 as a Tractarian village church. You are drawn to the chancel by the glowing ribs of the ceiling, and you find the

Chancel roof, St Michael's, Sowton.

walls are delicately stencilled, the floors covered in decorative tiles, as is the wall behind the painted wooden altar. There are Gothic porcelain Commandment Boards and a brass and iron communion rail. The fine stained glass by Willement includes a most striking west window showing St Michael against a deep blue background, not dissimilar to the colour to be found in a John Piper window at St Andrew's, Plymouth.

STAVERTON
St Paul de Lyon

2m/3km NW of Totnes

Staverton church dates from an edict giving directions for a larger church to be erected, issued by the Bishop of Exeter, Walter Stapledon, following his visit on 1st April 1314. The present building has a spacious and well-lit interior with a nave of five bays and two aisles. The powerful geometric tracery of the south aisle windows was designed by E. W. Godwin in 1858-60. The extensive chestnut-coloured screen was restored by Harry Hems in 1891-3. Opposite the porch there is an ancient yew tree over a thousand years of age.

TALATON
St James

6m/10km W of Honiton

Towers are dominant in the Devon landscape, proudly proclaiming the existence of a church – and village – and varying in character from the massive to the elegant, the sombre to the powerful. Many are Perpendicular in date and with their original statuary missing. An exception is the very handsome tower of Talaton, whose statues survived the destruction of the Reformation and the Civil War.

Built of Trap stone with Beer stone dressings, both from local quarries, the tower dates from the early fifteenth century. It rises in three stages, with plain stringcourse moulding at each level. It has pinnacles on all

St James, Talaton.

Facing page: John Glanville, St Eustachius, Tavistock.

four corners and a polygonal stair-turret, or Vice, which rises above the battlements. Just below, within niches in this turret, are the figures of some saints. On the four corners of the tower are statues of the Evangelists, while St Michael stands on the uppermost stage of the turret with the Virgin and Child in the niche below him.

The tower has a peal of six bells. The oldest of these, the tenor bell, was given by Johanne de Beauchamp, Countess of Warwick, who died in 1435.

TAVISTOCK
St Eustachius

13m/21km N of Plymouth

This large Perpendicular church has an especially spacious and stately interior. The nave with its north and south aisles of five bays, the chancel and outer south aisle (the Clothworkers Aisle) are early sixteenth century. It is lit by large four-light aisle windows which provide entrancing vistas.

Special features include a stained-glass window by Burne-Jones and William Morris (1876, north aisle) and monuments to John Fitz and his wife and son (1590) and John Glanville and wife (1600). The portly figure of Glanville lies recumbent in the manner of an oversize seal basking on an ice shelf; his wife kneels quite separate in front of him. Their portraits are exceptionally naturalistic.

At the south-west corner of the churchyard is a collection of slate gravestones, the oldest late eighteenth century. Cornish winged angels are amongst them.

TEIGNGRACE
St Peter & St Paul

2m/3km NW of Newton Abbot

This is a church like no other in the county: coloured two shades of cobalt blue, Strawberry Hill Gothic in style and cruciform with a shallow unlighted dome, perfectly circular. The mood is tranquil, harmonious and yet domestic – a frozen dream of eighteenth-century clarity.

The building originally dated from the fourteenth century, but in 1786 the Templers of nearby Stover Park had the courage to replace it with a fully fledged and handsome *à la mode* design. There is an eighteenth-century organ and a number of wall monuments of discreet taste; the Nelson Memorial (1805) is particularly handsome. In addition to the charming eighteenth-century font there is a dark copy of Van Dyck's *Pieta* painted by James Barry above the altar. A yew tree planted in 1788 stands before the west entrance to the church.

TEIGNMOUTH
St James

20m/32km S of Exeter

In Teignmouth and close by are two exceptional buildings: the Arts and Crafts church of St Peter at Shaldon, and St James's in the town. The latter has a delightful open and airy interior, very different from the east/west orientation of the normal Perpendicular building, and essentially egalitarian in spirit. It is certainly exhilarating to enter this remarkable church. The body of it is an octagon, within which a circle of slender clustered cast-iron piers supports the thin cast-iron rib vaulting, and a lantern which may have been inspired by the octagon of Ely Cathedral. It is a delightful and totally unexpected use of the new material. Before the close of the eighteenth century, cast iron had been employed in the construction of industrial buildings, but as far as I know, this was its first use in a church.

The designer was W. E. Rolfe, a pupil of Sir John Soane, but St James was built between 1817 and 1821 by the Exeter architect Andrew Patey. His plan included galleries on three

Looking up into the octagon, St James, Teignmouth.

sides (seating capacity for 1,500 people), but these were removed in 1891, with the exception of those in the organ gallery.

The original Norman foundation dates from 1268, and the church's squat but unforgettable red sandstone tower, the oldest structure in Teignmouth, now sits alongside the battlemented, octagonal form of the early nineteenth-century church.

Its interior holds a few features of interest. These include a mediaeval reredos, five bays of Decorated work with additional gold-coloured side panels on which are painted the Lord's Prayer, the Creed and the Commandments. There is also a muscular font and a pulpit dating from 1900.

TETCOTT
Holy Cross

5m/8km S of Holsworthy

It is luxuriously hot; July now. The harvest is in, the hedgerow grasses are bleached; the foxgloves have flowered, and there across the old, oaky Arscott park is the tower of Tetcott church with its cusped pinnacles, a delicate pale grey colour like a pearl.

It is mostly a thirteenth-century building, but the font is earlier, Norman. There are some rather weather-beaten bench ends in the nave, ten hanging lamps, and a framed list of rectors – 39 since 1310 – which add to the interest of this simple, deeply pastoral place. Note the little transept to the south of the nave with its four Arscott family memorials, the most splendid for John Arscott who died in 1675, and his wife, Gertrude, who died in 1699. Another, simpler, egg-shaped memorial is for the two wives of John Arscott who died in 1708. There is also a tablet to the last of the Arscotts. By all accounts, John Arscott (1718-88), was a larger than life character whose favourite, a man only four feet high, "hump-backed and misshapen", was a jester dwarf known as Black John. One of his less usual skills was the swallowing of live mice.

But it is not only the church which attracts the visitor to Tetcott: here is a place as romantic as the story of Sir Gawain and the Green Knight; a group of buildings – a barn, a brick granary, stables and a seventeenth-century manor house – as enchanted and enchanting as anywhere in England.

I returned the key to the elderly churchwarden, Norman Pearce, who lives in the village, and told him I admired how well the church was being maintained. "Thank you," he responded, "but there's so few of us left to do it." It was not the first time I had heard that lament.

THROWLEIGH
St Mary the Virgin

6m/10km SE of Okehampton
On the day of our visit the churchyard was full of life with swallows, preoccupied, overworked, not to say frantic, flying backwards and forwards into the porch to feed their hungry offspring.

By contrast, the interior of the church was a scene of utter tranquillity, radiant with light and of an unsophisticated beauty. There are wagon roofs to the chancel and aisles, granite window tracery and piers, carved oak bosses, a handsome pulpit, a restored rood-screen and two windows by Sir Ninian

Comper (1912). The Easter Sepulchre in the sanctuary and an ornate chancel doorway on the south side of the church are also beautiful.

The rustic atmosphere of these granite Dartmoor churches makes them amongst the loveliest in the county.

TIVERTON
St George

Fore Street
The church was designed by John James, the architect of St George, Hanover Square in London (1712-24), and dates from 1714. Originally built for the town's Dissenters, it has had a chequered history but was completed in 1723-33. Its clock tower, bell and turret were added in 1737.

The interior, one large, symmetrical, unimpeded but galleried space, approximates to Sir Christopher Wren's model town church, St James's, Piccadilly (1683) which its architect instanced as "beautiful and convenient" and the best solution he had found to the problem of enabling a large congregation "to hear distinctly, and to see the Preacher". This is an admirable description of St George's, Tiverton.

The interior, if harmonious, is rather standardised. The panelling around the chancel, the balusters of the altar-rails and the general air of a restrained decorum are attractive, but the overall effect is plain, not to say dullish. Far from dull, however, is the over-dominant east window – a stained-glass study depicting St Andrew, installed in 1845 – which in the right place could be a handsome feature. Here it is seriously out of place, its spirit totally at odds with that of the church as a whole.

After visiting over 200 Gothic churches, I had looked forward to seeing Devon's only classical one, but confess to a certain disappointment.

TORQUAY
St Luke

St Luke's Road, Warren Hill

An atmosphere of cheerful jubilation greets the visitor to this highly coloured interior, but this, I suspect, may have more to do with paint than architecture, The church was an early work of Arthur Blomfield (1863). It has a pleasant interior with short iron columns and an apsed chancel roof, which has been painted with panels depicting angels and the Benedicite. These are by Heaton, Butler & Bayne (who also provided the good glass in that part of the building). The present decor (which includes the brightly painted red iron columns) was introduced by Prebendary W. H. Ryder-Jones after a fire in the 1960s. There is a delightful marble font in the north-west corner of the church.

Painted roof in the chancel apse, St Luke's, Torquay.

TRENTISHOE
St Peter

2m/3km W of Lynton

This is one of the most delightful and unexpected churches in Devon; not perhaps great architecture but an inimitable building in a sensational setting. It is tucked away at the head of a densely wooded combe, less than half a mile from the sea and on the edge of Exmoor – it is very remote.

As so often, it is the simplicities which speak to me more deeply than the splendours of the richer churches.

The church is tiny and would have been even smaller before the present chancel was added in 1868. It has a castellated toy-tower (1681) with two bells, and an interior nineteenth-century in mood – whitewashed walls, dark woodwork, candles, simple choir stalls and a musicians' gallery complete with a hole in the front of its balcony for the spike of the bass viol. On the altar, an open bible, two candlesticks and vases of flowers.

There are neither transepts nor aisles. It feels well used, maybe a trifle shabby. There is a monthly service and 27 in the parish. No village as such, but a scatter of buildings around the church.

TRUSHAM
St Michael

2m/3km NE of Chudleigh

This small and intimate fifteenth-century interior, full of character, with its three-bay granite arcade, simple wagon roof and dark wood screen (largely carved by Herbert Read), is an attractive place – not easily forgotten. It has a shadowy brown chancel with a decoratively painted ceiled wagon roof, and a reredos of 1865, flanked by Commandments in Gothic niches – Victorian design at its most appealing. There is a painted angel on its south wall, a pillar

Altar at St Peter's, Trentishoe.

piscina, and three windows by Clayton and Bell in the nave.

Unusually, its memorials are not of stone, but painted. The largest consists of portraits of John Stooke and his wife (1697) in an architectural framework painted to simulate marble; the oldest commemorates the Stapehill family, all kneeling. It dates from the late sixteenth century.

Views of the landscape from the churchyard are beautiful. Trusham lies in the western foothills of Haldon where they fall to the Teign valley.

UFFCULME

St Mary

8m/12km E of Tiverton

A large, spacious, optimistic interior, mainly of the fifteenth century, but now proudly but characterlessly modernised with carpets and reordered altar and pews. The pulpit dates

from 1719; there is an extensive early fifteenth-century screen, the longest in Devon; but it is the monumental sculpture in the Walrond chapel which first catches the eye. Here, on a tomb chest are the coarsely carved and painted life-sized busts of a man, a woman and a boy, c.1650. No less astonishing is the reclining figure of a gentleman in armour. He is wearing a full-bottomed wig and is lying (most uncomfortably, I'd have thought) on a windowsill. This commemorates another Walrond, and dates from c.1700.

However, the *pièce de résistance* is the chancel, a dream of bold Puginesque Gothic. It was rebuilt and refitted in 1843 by John Hayward, who also added the outer south aisle and rebuilt the spire. His fittings, a stone Gothic reredos, a plaster barrel vault and other Tractarian features, have been painted with an almost fairground exuberance which brings joy into the church.

Busts of boy and woman, St Mary's, Uffculme.

UGBOROUGH

St Peter

3m/4km E of Ivybridge

If you approach from the north, downhill, you will suddenly see the impressive tower looming up through the trees. When you reach the handsome square, you find it dominated by the church on the higher side. A church existed in Ugborough before 1121, but all that remains of that building is the present nave and probably the old and mutilated sandstone font, with some of its palmette decoration. During the rectorship of William de Kylkenny (1301-29) the church was enlarged; probably the beautiful ceiling of the north aisle dates from this time. The second boss from the west shows a farrier with his anvil, tongs and horseshoe, reminding us of St Eloy, the patron saint of farriers and goldsmiths. There is also a sow

with a litter of eight. The central boss is of a woman with two small dogs.

The interior has a pleasant, comfortable quality, cared for and well lit. It is long and low-vaulted, with an arcade of octagonal piers composed of grey and pinky-grey stones. There is a white-painted pulpit and a cut-down screen across the nave and aisles. Its wainscoting, with 32 painted panels c.1525, remains complete.

Delightful, too, if more ephemeral, was a garland of summer flowers – clematis, daisies, carnations – woven into the decorated stone border of the south porch door.

UPTON HELLIONS

St Mary

2m/3km N of Crediton

If only two miles from Crediton, this wonderful church lies in deep, forgotten,

Angel on the tower screen, St Peter's, Ugborough.

beautiful red sandstone country. The narrow, winding lanes add to the sense of complete remoteness. The church is surrounded by a few houses, but there is no village.

The first sensation on opening its doorway is of stunned surprise; this church, one sees, is characterised by an aesthetic of dignity rather than of splendour. It is an old foundation – the first mass was chanted within its walls on August 15th 1227 – but the present building is of several later periods: Perpendicular, Tudor, Victorian. There is a simple Norman font, some sinewy wagon roofs, plain plastered walls, and clear-glass windows providing lovely views of the surrounding countryside. There is also a bench end on which a lion couchant has been carved (see page 206), and a sombrely coloured early seventeenth-century wall monument (all chalky greys and fawns).

But here it is the total ensemble which stirs. This is a place of prayer and silence, of unsophisticated grace, of the profoundest refreshment whatever your faith. The presence of a King James Bible open on the lectern, and the gifts of poetry offered to visitors (even a poem by the contemporary and little known American poet, Mary Oliver) added to the sacredness of this sanctuary.

A week before, I had been walking in the cathedral at Chartres (with which no helpful comparison with St Mary's can be made), but the latter's unsophisticated poetry was not dwarfed by the remembrance. Both, I felt, had in different degrees the power to lead us through the negation of outer, normal, transient busy-ness to the place that is at the still point.

WASHFORD PYNE

St Peter

9m/15km W of Tiverton

This isolated little church, hardly larger than a chapel, is in beautiful, remote countryside. It has a broach spire and a darkly attractive exterior made up of different stones: local brownstone, purple-red sandstone and touches of ochre Ham Hill stone; clearly the architect, Robert Medley Fulford, had an eye

St Peter's, Washford Pyne.

for colour. The same sensitivity is apparent in its modest, atmospheric and well-proportioned interior, designed in 1883-4. There are quirky touches here: inventively designed windows and a beguiling mood of unpretentious rusticity.

Indeed St Peter's, with its polished brass (such as the vertical barley-sugar stands for the paraffin lamps, Puginesque candlesticks on the pulpit, and little organ with its decorated pipes) is as intimately consistent in its style as, say, Molland is in a Georgian one. On the day of my visit, the quiet climax of this engaging interior was the attractively presented white altar with its brass fittings: a cross, candlesticks and vases.

WELCOMBE

St Nectan

5m/8km S of Hartland

The hillside on which St Nectan's sits overlooks the Atlantic, the sea dove-grey and calm on this late January morning, the day cold, brilliant, cloudlesss, with snowdrops flowering in the hedges.

Once a mediaeval chapel of Hartland Abbey, this small church has a low, stumpy tower and is surrounded by a sloping graveyard filled with beautifully lettered slate gravestones: although Welcombe is in Devon, their style, like the place, is distinctly Cornish. The aisleless interior has north and south transepts and an early fourteenth-century screen, perhaps the earliest in Devon. The lectern and pulpit are also notable; the former Jacobean, the latter with restored early Renaissance panels. Old stones are used for paving, and there are excellent modern light fittings, probably the best I have seen. The feeling throughout the church is neighbourly, a womb of comfort for its community.

On the day of my visit the church was enlivened with light reflected from the sea.

Rev. R. S. Hawker, the poet and antiquary, was curate here for thirty years, holding the living with neighbouring Morwenstow from 1851. Across the road is St Nectan's Well.

WEST OGWELL

Dedication unknown

3m/4km SW of Newton Abbot

Approached by winding, deep-set lanes, West Ogwell has an atmosphere of remote obscurity, which is strange because of its proximity to one of Devon's largest (and ugliest) towns.

The origins of the church are not known but West Ogwell is essentially mediaeval in fabric (c.1300). However, following the rebuilding of the Manor House in 1790, box pews, benches and a plaster vault were installed. The church is a rarity in having escaped both late mediaeval Perpendicular remodelling and radical Victorian restoration.

Its interior has an almost Quakerish simplicity. When that fine chronicler of Devon's churches, John Stubb, photographed it c.1900, the wagon roof was plastered, and the Commandments, the Lord's Prayer and Creed were displayed on panels behind the communion table. There was also a reading desk and box pews extending into the chancel. The box pews, simple Jacobean pulpit and curved communion rails are still in place, but some things have disappeared. Nonetheless, this is a wonderful place, unspoilt and poetic. The church is in the care of the Churches Conservation Trust.

WEST PUTFORD

St Stephen

8m/12km N of Holsworthy

The present church dates from the early fourteenth century. The only object predating this period is the Norman font but

The church at West Ogwell.

there are also several later features of interest including the oak beams in the north transept ceiling with their carved wooden heads and a water stoup set into the wall beside the south porch. The tower, wintry in mood, was added during the late fifteenth century, the approximate date of the Barnstaple tiles on the chancel floor. The church has an eighteenth-century pulpit, communion rails with twisted balusters, an exceptionally heavy wooden entrance door (dated 1620) with knocker, and a series of slate tombstones dating from 1642, 1663, 1681, 1710 and 1711 in the church. There is also a Royal coat of arms of 1714.

I have always been attracted by the modesty, loneliness and piety of this church and its isolated setting.

WESTLEIGH
St Peter

4m/6km E of Bideford

The village lies on a hillside overlooking the beautiful and sweeping Taw estuary between Bideford and Barnstaple. I had some difficulty getting into the church, but eventually the husband of one of the churchwardens kindly accompanied me. While I looked around, Mr Baltesz continued his preparations for the forthcoming carol concert, for which over a hundred candles and a large Christmas tree were already in place.

It's a medium-sized but spacious church with a wide nave and chancel (five granite nave piers long), good slate and tile floors, numerous carved bench ends, some wall monuments and much Victorian glass. Average, you might say, but on the morning I visited, it felt both dignified and handsome; not spectacular, but a comfortable home for village worship.

WOOLACOMBE
St Sabinus

8m/12km SW of Ilfracombe

Woolacombe Bay is a glorious site: a three-mile-long stretch of golden sand, a silent winter sea and, on this late December morning, an air of desolation about the place – only one distant surfer and two scampering dogs, with their owner taking her daily stroll on the beach. Apart from the majestic sweep of the bay and W. D. Caröe's church on the hill above the village, there is nothing of distinction here. But both are very special.

Built in 1910 out of Devonian red sandstone with traces of iron quarried from within the parish, St Sabinus is a delightful if highly idiosyncratic version of a free Arts and Crafts Gothic. Like this architect's other Devon church, St David's in Exeter, with which the Woolacombe church shares certain features – an extremely wide five-bay nave and narrow passage-like aisles with low cusped windows – St Sabinus enjoys comfortable proportions and a friendly, welcoming atmosphere. It is smaller than St David's, but also exceptionally well built.

Major differences include the nave's pitched wooden roof, the chancel's curved wooden one, and the prevailing colour of the interior: an unusual, milky, umberish burnt sienna, which sets the warm human tone. Note Caröe's inventive use of space and his design of the sedilia in the chancel.

Slate headstones, West Putford.

YARNSCOMBE
St Andrew

6m/10km NE of Great Torrington

A delightful church both inside and out, characterised by purity and calm. On the afternoon of my visit, a strong and frosty light shone through its plain, latticed, south-aisle windows, splashing the walls of its bare whitewashed interior with pools of gold.

There is a stately tower, a four-bay granite arcade, old ceiled wagon roofs and two low Perpendicular recesses (the one in the chancel probably an Easter Sepulchre). There is a beautiful late mediaeval angel in the east window of the south aisle.

Except for the excited chattering of birds it was very, very still. According to the guide, the name of the village derives from the Domesday Book of 1086: "Hernescombe, the valley of the eagles." The "eagles" were probably buzzards, which still breed in the parish.

YELVERTON
St Paul

8m/12km N of Plymouth

Standing on the wide grassy plateau where the moor roads meet is another church by Nicholson and Corlette, who designed the splendid St Matthew, Chelston, in Torquay. This is simpler, and its dark grey exterior somewhat daunting, with a battlemented tower and steeply-pitched roofs.

Inside, however, all is light Ham Hill stone and airy space. The rough-cut pillars have sharp edges, giving a modern air to the space they inhabit. The most pleasing feature is the cheerfully painted wooden roofs, of nave and lean-to aisles. There is a jolly font carved with rhythmical leaping fish.

On my visit, on Maundy Thursday, the Last Supper was laid out in the nave, on a long table with white cloths, just waiting for the arrival of the disciples and Leonardo da Vinci.

Inscription on the roof, Yarnscombe.

Facing page: Ham Hill stone pillars in St Paul's, Yelverton.

OTHER PLACES
OF WORSHIP

The county of Devon has been prominent in its contribution to religious dissent. According to Hoskins, when Puritanism gained the upper hand during the Civil War and Commonwealth and set out to eliminate Episcopacy, about one third of the clergy of Devon were ejected from their livings, mostly from the rural parishes. The Act of Uniformity (1662) barred the Puritan clergy from their retention of their livings, and of the 2,000 clergy who resigned as a result of this Act, at least 132 were to be found in Devon. Nonconformity was particularly strong in the towns, and the growth of dissent was greatly encouraged by the increasing laxity of the established Church. The subsequent emergence of dissenting congregations, mostly of the Presbyterian order, left a legacy of chapels which few counties can rival. According to my calculations there are well over 300 Nonconformist places of worship in the county.

Of the 205 chapels and meeting houses in Devon listed by Christopher Stell in his *Inventory of Nonconformist Chapels and Meeting Houses in South-West England*, the Royal Commission on the Historical Monuments of England selected nine as especially 'worthy of preservation'. These include: the Jesu Street Chapel, Ottery St Mary (of the late seventeenth century but subsequently altered); the former Baptist Chapel at Loughwood, Dalwood (c.1700) described below; the Congregational Chapel, Chulmleigh (1710); the recently restored Salem Chapel, East Budleigh (1719); the former Nonconformist chapel known as George's Meeting House, Exeter, (1760); the Wesleyan Chapel, Lana, Pancrasweek (1838); the Congregational chapel and almshouses, Exmouth (1811); the Friends meeting house, Spiceland, near Culmstock (1815); and the Great Meeting House in Bridgeland Street in Bideford of 1859. Of these, I have seen but five.

These are attractive buildings, especially those of the eighteenth century which have a clear-headed lucidity of design. The buildings themselves are invariably relatively plain, with an auditorium chiefly designed for the purpose of preaching the Gospel. The windows are usually of clear glass; no dim religious mystery here. Although unadorned, even austere, the architecture of Nonconformism can yet possess a quiet radiance and beauty of its own.

This is untrue of the Catholic church architecture, which emerged from the great revival of faith which followed the Catholic Relief Act of 1830, and brought with it a hugely ambitious programme of church building. Our Lady Help of Christians (R. C.) in Torquay (see page 90) is an example of the scale, the confidence and splendour of this revival.

Facing page: Point-in-View Chapel, Exmouth.

Non-conformist architecture

by Dr David Keep

Nonconformist preaching began in barns and warehouses. The earliest chapels were founded during the Commonwealth by Independents and Quakers. Some included a baptistery for immersion. These buildings were usually in a domestic or agricultural style. Under the Clarendon Code of 1662 dissenting chapels had to be five miles from a town, hence the sites of Loughwood at Dalwood (see below), Salem in East Budleigh, Gulliford in Woodbury (where only the graveyard survives) and at Moreleigh near Totnes (which is now a house).

The Toleration Act of 1689 allowed freedom of worship to orthodox dissenters; meeting houses had to be licensed. Wealthy Presbyterian congregations built increasingly fine classical houses: George's Meeting in South Street, Exeter (now restored as a Wetherspoon pub) is an example of one of these. It was built in 1760, one of six meeting houses in the city. Old dissent split over the divinity of Jesus and many meeting houses became Unitarian, e.g. Sidmouth (1710/1884) and Cullompton (1698/1912), though this was technically illegal until 1813. Other meeting houses became Congregationalist as the Presbyterian organisation collapsed, e.g. Lady Glenorchy's, Exmouth, rebuilt in 1866. However, the Baptists avoided the controversy and are still using some old chapels. These include Bradninch (1832), Budleigh Salterton (1844/1877) and South Street, Exeter, rebuilt in 1823.

The diminutive Point-in-View Chapel in Exmouth was a private evangelical foundation with almshouses built in 1811 (now United Reformed) for the conversion of the Jews beside A la Ronde (1798), now a house belonging to the National Trust, like Loughwood Meeting House.

Methodism began in 1738 as a revival of the Church of England. John Wesley was compelled to license his buildings as meeting houses. These were cheaper than the Presbyterian; the best had a stone-faced façade with common bricks for the side walls, and most were rebuilt at least once. He purchased the subsequently twice rebuilt Mint in Exeter from the first Unitarian secession. Windsor Square, Exmouth, now Free Church of England, was replaced in 1897 by the Gothic Tower Street with a spire and truncated transepts. The old South Brent chapel exists as a cottage behind those opposite the 1840 replacement. The early nineteenth-century Methodist chapel in Buckfastleigh is a typical 'Messiah' chapel, with full galleries and a modern foyer. Buckfast (1882), modernised in 1936, coincided with the re-foundation of the Abbey and is always open. Scoriton had the new chapel built alongside the old in 1904, as did Lympstone, a rare former Primitive Methodist. Sampford Peverell was built in 1806 but has had the roof raised and a gallery inserted. Some villages used to have as many as two or three Methodist denominations.

The Oxford Movement led to further dissent. St John's, Bridgetown, Totnes (1832/1980) was independent, though now Anglican. The Free Church of England survives in Exeter, Torquay and Exmouth. Christchurch, Woodbury (1851), a plain brick box, was modernised by the

Brethren in 1969 and 2003. An interesting development was the sale of the Gothic Grosvenor Chapel in Barnstaple by the Brethren to the County Council and the rebuilding of the former railway goods shed as a worship centre in the 1990s.

There is a lot of nonconformist/suburban Gothic in Devon. The Methodist church in Wilder Road, Ilfracombe (1898) has an extraordinary window to Solomon as builder. Exmouth Baptist and principal Brethren are Gothic. Smaller chapels avoided stone façades and were simple hall style until the 1950s.

Loughwood Meeting House.

Two chapels

AYSHFORD

Ayshford Chapel; no dedication

8m/12km E of Tiverton

This small, former private chapel is in the grounds of Ayshford Court. It stands in a field within sight and sound of two major roads. Notwithstanding this disturbance, I love this place. I love its unexpectedness, its serenity and romantic mediaevalism. In fact the building reminds me of David Jones's painting of the Chapel Perilous, the mystical home of the Holy Grail. On the day I visited, no grail was to be found, only many, many staring eyes – a large huddle of inquisitive sheep blocked my advance into the field.

The architecture of the chapel does not reveal its date of origin, but does imply a considerable restoration of the building in the fifteenth century. It has a charming interior restored by the Friends of Friendless Churches, who painted the walls with a wonderful salmon-pink limewash. The building has a wagon roof, a painted mediaeval cusped screen (red and gold on a predominantly blue background), and some atmospheric Gothic Revival glass designed and made by the stained-glass artist John Toms (1813-1867) of Wellington in Somerset, dating from 1848. Its floor is tiled and the entrance door has an attractive hinge in the form of a large *fleur de lys*. There is a wall monument to John Ayshford, 1689, and another to Henry Ayshford, who died in 1666 aged one year nine months. The key holder is Mr T. G. Kelland (Tel 01884 820271).

DALWOOD

Loughwood Meeting House

4m/7km W of Axminster

A typical and easily accessible example of a Nonconformist building is the Loughwood Meeting House near Axminster which is virtually in the farmyard of Loughwood Farm. It was first mentioned in 1653 when a congregation in the village of Kilmington, some two miles to the south-east, sought refuge from persecution in a remoter place, the Lough Wood, then an area of dense woodland. The present Meeting House, dating from c.1700, still lies down a grassy track and amongst fields and trees; it is a simple, rubble-walled, thatched building with clear-glass windows. Inside there is one large room furnished with a high-set pulpit approached by steps, unvarnished pine box pew and a gallery for the players of stringed instruments who accompanied the hymns – their music rests are still in place, and in one position the book rest has been cut away to accommodate the bass viol. Under the floorboards there is an all-important baptismal pool, whose water was obtained from a nearby spring. There is also stabling, a fireplace and a simple kitchen.

Loughwood Meeting House and burial ground once served as the rallying point for the East Devon Baptists, in the cruel days of persecution before the passing of the Acts of Indulgence (1687) and Toleration (1689) which permitted Nonconformists to worship freely and openly.

SOME
IMPORTANT
FEATURES

BELLS

Steeples are rare in Devon but towers are ubiquitous, and in these as often as not there are bells. Devon has more towers than any other administrative county in Britain, and more bells too – about 2,800. Tiverton, Chulmleigh, Tavistock, Totnes, Modbury, have exceptional bells. North Molton, with a ring of six, is also very fine, while the cathedral has the second heaviest bells in the world hung for ringing full-cycle.

My informant is Reverend Prebendary Scott, who was the Exeter Diocese consultant on bells for many years, and the co-author of a major study of the county's towers and bells, recently published; he has, he tells me, climbed nearly all of Devon's 300 church towers and examined over 3,000 bells. "Many were cast in the eighteenth century when Devonians took up the art of ringing in earnest. Devon's oldest bells date from before 1340. The oldest to be rung full circle is at Peters Marland, which was cast by a man who is known to have been working in the early 1300s. It has the handsomest lettering in Latin." Bells had carried inscriptions from an early stage; stately Latin mottoes on mediaeval bells, but English rhyming couplets in the seventeenth century: "I to the church the living call/ And to the grave do summon all."

Above: Jill Newton, bell-ringer, Lympstone.
Facing page: Bell ropes, Dowland.

BENCH ENDS

It was the growing length of sermons that made fixed pews popular from the fourteenth century. Until then the congregation had stood or knelt, as they do to this day in Russian, Greek and Armenian Christian churches. Only the old or sick sat down, on stone benches round the wall – the origin of the phrase 'the weak go to the wall'.

The Devon bench end is a rectangular block of oak whose squared top rises a little, if at all, above the back of the seat. Often in the fifteenth century the outer surface was richly carved with animals, heads, emblems of the Passion, flowers, hagiology, mermaids, tracery, vines, and instruments of the wool trade, amongst many other designs. Unlike the sophisticated carving of the screens, bench ends often have simple bold patterns. Two great figures at Colebrooke, of a wild man and a fool, are particularly powerful. In Lapford (1540) newly imported Renaissance motifs are found beside traditional Gothic forms. The largest collection of bench-ends is at Braunton with 84 examples (1560-93), High Bickington has 70 (c.1520-40) and East Budleigh 63 examples (1537), including a fine ship in the parish where Sir Walter Raleigh was born.

Some box pews survive from the Georgian period, when the nave pulpit became the focal point of the service, and the communion wine was often port. Comfort was the watchword, pew rents were paid, the pews sometimes upholstered. Those of the greatest families sometimes even had a fireplace. In Victorian times, the Tractarians and the Ecclesiologists railed against all this comfort, and as the focus of worship returned to the high altar, most box pews were swept away. Some remain in Devon churches, the most spectacular being at Parracombe, and there is a rare Jacobean family pew at Holcombe Rogus.

Above left: Upton Hellions. Above right: East Budleigh. Facing page: Northlew.

CAPITALS

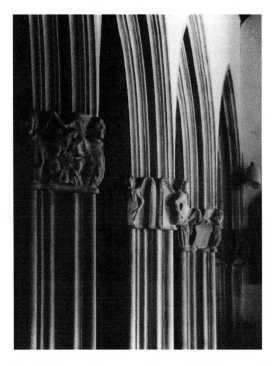

Most of the piers we see in Devon churches date from the Perpendicular period, the time of the great rebuild in the county. The moulding of their shafts is partly determined by the stone being used. Where it is granite, hard to carve, a simpler form is used. Columns of Beer stone allowed a more elaborate design, which Pevsner describes as wave moulding, giving the effect of clustered piers in ambitious examples like Bradninch, Broadhembury and Woodbury. Beer stone also allowed the carving of capitals. The characteristic Devon form is a band of large leaves, occasionally with acorns amongst them, and this is what you find in the majority of our Perpendicular churches. Occasionally, however, there will be figure carving, which usually takes the form of angels holding shields, to be found at Broadclyst, East Budleigh, and memorably at Alphington. Tiverton, a great wool church, has sheep on the capitals, and Cullompton, another, shows implements of the trade, such as teazles and shears. At Stockleigh Pomeroy there are mermaids, at Wolborough a pig, and splendidly, at East Ogwell, a crocodile crawling round the capital of one pillar. Dolphins are found at the Arts and Crafts church of St Matthew, Torquay.

Above top: Sowton. Below left: Tools of wool trade, Cullompton. Below right: Ashcombe. Facing page: Above left: Crocodile, East Ogwell. Above right: Stockleigh Pomeroy. Below left: St Matthew, Torquay. Below right: Sowton.

CHURCHYARDS

One definition of a 'local' is someone who has at least three generations of forbears in the graveyard. Their worn tombstones, lichen-mottled and leaning, make the country churchyard a place of quiet beauty.

But these were not always areas of arcadian repose. Before they became burial grounds, churchyards were venues for cock-fighting, quoins, ninepins, ball games and fencing. In the mediaeval period they were also used for dancing, plays and drunken events called 'church ales'. Fairs were held in them, and travelling merchants set up their stalls.

Unlike, say, Gloucestershire, or even parts of neighbouring Cornwall, Devon did not have a tradition of superb letter carvers, and individual tombstones are rarely remarkable. But their atmosphere makes a special contribution to a village or townscape, most romantic when the grasses are not too enthusiastically cut, and ruined only when the gravestones are removed from the mounds they mark, and lined up against the wall like prisoners waiting to be shot.

Another advantage of planned mowing is, as Francesca Greenoak reports in her book on churchyards, the beauty that comes with the wildflowers. She recounts how she visited St Swithun's, Littleham, on May Day, "an experience I shall not forget . . . There were all the plants I had come to expect in a good traditional churchyard: bluebells, red campion, primroses, the churchyard pink primrose, speedwells, stitchwort and lady's smock. In taller patches of vegetation, hemp agrimony was coming up along with columbines, cow parsley and

foxgloves. There were ramsons, dog's mercury, woodrush, and the clear blue of bugle flowers."

Older than the gravestones, older than the churches, are many of the great yews that cast their shade upon them. The 1,100-year-old yew at Plymtree provided 'palms' for the Palm Sunday procession, according to a sixteenth-century text. The Payhembury Yew could date back 2,000 years. These ancient, sacred trees, "produced too slowly ever to decay", as Wordsworth said, mark a holy place, Christian symbols of everlasting life, trees that seem themselves to be immortal.

DOORS & DOORWAYS

Doorways with decoration are mainly Norman, and some 40 remain as entrances to Devon churches. They were often preserved and reused even when the church was rebuilt. Zigzag and beakhead patterns are characteristic. The elaborate doorway of St John's, Paignton, has saltire crosses, zigzag and scalloped capitals in alternating red and white stone; at East Worlington the zigzag rests on a beast's head; and there are fine beakheads to be seen at Shebbear and at Bishopsteignton, which also boasts a large fierce bird. Few decorative tympana remain, but a good one is at Bishopsteignton showing the Adoration of the Magi, and there is a lovely twelfth-century scene of Daniel in the Lions Den at Down St Mary.

The south door at Lapford is probably Norman, and there are heavy mediaeval doors complete with their original ironwork – door handles, nails and hinges. I have seen these at Honeychurch, Ipplepen, Knowstone, North Molton, Sampford Courtenay and Satterleigh, among other places. By far the most striking is to be found at St Saviour's, Dartmouth, where the two rampant Lions of King Edward I guard the Tree of Life and the entrance to the church.

Above: Bishopsteignton. Top: West doorway, Below: Tympanum on south wall.
Facing page: Folding door, Sampford Courtenay.

FONTS

There is just one Saxon font in Devon, at Dolton, and that is made up of fragments of a cross. The county has a remarkable number of Norman fonts – nearly 150. Their shapes are square, circular, eggcup, goblet, tub-shaped, all in stone, some granite, some red sandstone, some in Purbeck marble, some in Beer stone, like the outstanding font at Alphington, richly carved. In the South Hams, there is a series decorated with the same features, palmette scroll, cable moulding and zigzag in different combinations. Most engaging are the fonts with figures, often primitive, the star of which is at Luppitt, vigorously carved on all four sides from granite. More sophisticated is the single great beast on the font at Topsham. Mediaeval Devon fonts do not compare with those of some other counties, but certain Victorian architects brought a renewed imagination which reached its apogee in Butterfield's dazzling font of Devon and Sicilian marble at Ottery St Mary.

From top: Cheriton Bishop, Sampford Courtenay, 18th-century cover at Cruwys Morchard, Ottery St Mary. Facing page: Honeychurch.
Page 216: Above: Detail of Luppitt font. Below left: Topsham. Below right: Dolton. Page 217: Hartland.

LECTERNS & PULPITS

After the Reformation, the Word became the dominant feature of church services. Reading-desks, which in the Middle Ages stood in the chancel, were moved into the nave near the pulpit, and in 1604, the year the King James Bible was commissioned, they were made compulsory. In its most splendid form the lectern takes the shape of an eagle, with the Holy Book resting on its outspread wings. There is a fine Elizabethan eagle at Ashcombe, and at Ottery St Mary possibly the earliest eagle lectern in England, given by Bishop Grandison. A fifteenth-century brass eagle at Bovey Tracey seems to have been made in East Anglia. The Victorians also took up the eagle theme, although Butterfield, as usual, had his original ideas, in the form of a lectern of glittering Devon marble at Babbacombe.

In the abbeys, pulpits date from as early as the twelfth century, but were not generally used in churches for another 300 years. Devon has some local and unusual early examples. At Dittisham there is a stone pulpit, on a palm-like foot, deeply carved with leaves and naive figures of brightly coloured saints. There are only 60 mediaeval stone pulpits in all England, and eleven of these are in Devon, four of them nearby, and of a similar pattern. Of mediaeval wooden pulpits, the outstanding one is at Coldridge, a delicate piece of fretwork carving in pale wood. Only two eighteenth-century three-decker pulpits survive, at Branscombe and Molland on Exmoor. There are some good Victorian pulpits, and from 1910 a wonderful Arts and Crafts pulpit of marble and alabaster at Shaldon.

Above right: Flemish carving on lectern at Newton St Cyres. Above left: 18th-century pulpit, South Tawton.
Facing page: Elizabethan lectern, Ashcombe.

MONUMENTS

Knights and their ladies on mediaeval tomb chests are invariably lying down, their feet resting on appropriate animals, their heads often supported by angels. Outside the cathedral, where Bishop Branscombe reigns supreme, Devon does not have a hugely distinguished collection of early recumbent sculpture. Bere Ferrers has one of the best examples, a lady with a wimple lying elegantly next to a crossed-legged knight. One of the earliest effigies in England with crossed legs is to be found at Atherington, another fine piece of carving, if rather worn.

The great period for Devon monumental sculpture was the Elizabethan and Jacobean. By now the figures are showing more signs of life, raising themselves on an elbow, kneeling in front of the tomb, or memorably at Newton St Cyres and Eggesford standing to greet the visitor. These were secular monuments, designed to celebrate not just the saints, bishops and aristocracy, but newly wealthy Elizabethan merchants and administrators. The more I travelled round the churches of Devon, the more impressed I became with these vigorous and confident pieces of sculpture. At Berry Pomeroy a wonderfully comic tomb of the Seymour family shows three members lying one above the other, leaning nonchalantly on their elbows. Several great men have a wife either side, and many pious children kneel dutifully at their feet. The wives sometimes sit resting their chins on a hand, looking slightly fed up. These families bring a sense of affectionate domesticity to Devon churches.

From the Napoleonic period, we find a monument at Buckland Monachorum to Admiral Heathfield, the hero of Gibraltar, which has in the background reliefs of sea battles and a kiln

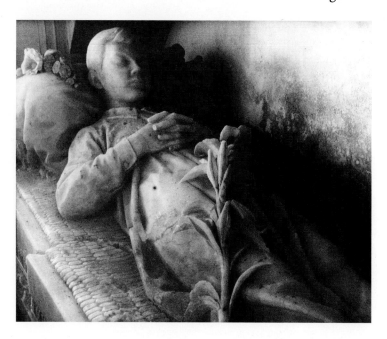

for making cannonballs. There are two remarkable standing figures, Lady Rachel Fane of 1680 by Balthazar Burman at Tawstock, which has the finest collection of monuments in the county, and Sir William Pole of 1746 by Richard Hayward at Shute. In both cases their clothing is wonderfully realised. The monuments of Devon churches could really do with a book all of their own.

Above: Monument to Robert 'Tito' Harvey, Harberton. Facing page: Leach tomb, 1630, Cadeleigh. Page 222: Top left & right, from monuments at Tawstock. Below, Richard Bluett, 1614, Holcombe Rogus. Page 223: Heathfield monument, Buckland Monachorum.

ROOD-SCREENS

Screens are the glories of Devon churches, intricately carved timber constructions stretching across the front of the chancel, and often across the whole width of the interior. Most date from the fifteenth and sixteenth centuries, and were the work of local carpenters – we even know their names at Atherington. The rood crosses that they carried have all gone, casualties of the Reformation, and only a Golgotha at Cullompton, used as the base for the cross, survives, uniquely in England. Gone, too, are most of the lofts and parapets that surmounted Devon screens, except at Atherington and in a couple of reconstructions, but the wonderful ribbed coving remains, sometimes decorated with Renaissance medallions and putti, as at Lapford. The most detailed carving is to be found in the cornice, an intricate band of vines, fruit, leaves and trailing stems, sometimes with birds eating the grapes, in flowing patterns of great beauty. The craftsmanship is astonishing. The wainscot was often painted with figures of saints, sometimes defaced (literally) by agents of the Reformation. At Bridford there are carved figures, and in this case their faces have been sliced off. Recent conservation work has revealed original paintwork at Bridford and on several other screens, for these were brightly decorated objects, and still are in many cases. Some 140 mediaeval rood-screens remain, of which more than 50 are vaulted. Only Somerset and Norfolk can boast such a rich heritage.

The great study of screens, *Roodscreens and Roodlofts* by Bligh Bond and Dom Camm, was published in 1909, and makes 11 different classifications of Devon screens, including the French/Moorish influence seen at Colebrooke and nearby churches. Pevsner divides standard screens into two types, distinguished by their tracery, and then identifies three further local types. But however you classify them, the rood-screens of Devon appear to us as imaginative works of art of great local craftsmanship.

Above: Early 16th-century figures on the wainscot, Bovey Tracey. Facing page: Cornices at Berry Pomeroy (top), Buckland in the Moor (below). Page 226: Fan-vaulted coving, Bradninch. Page 227: Eve being expelled from Paradise on the wainscot, early 16th century, Bradninch.

ROOF BOSSES

A good pair of binoculars is recommended for those who wish to enjoy roof bosses. The number in Devon's churches has not been calculated, but it is certainly large. The Cathedral has over 370, dating from the last quarter of the thirteenth century to the second half of the fourteenth, and they are amongst the most important in England. Some parish churches have nearly as many: 210 in Tavistock, 197 in North Tawton. In his brilliant book *Roof Bosses in Mediaeval Churches*, C. J. P. Cave lists (and sometimes reproduces) dozens of the county's bosses: a blacksmith at Ugborough and a sow with piglets, angels at Buckland Monachorum, rabbits at North Bovey, a Green Man at Sampford Courtenay. Originally pre-Christian, the Green Man is a symbol of our unity with the natural world, and was absorbed into mediaeval culture. Devon is especially rich in examples. There are over 60 in the Cathedral and they are to be found in over a hundred parish churches.

One of the best collections of roof bosses is at Ottery St Mary, of saints and bishops, including the church's patron, Bishop Grandison (see page 74).

Top: Bishop Grandison, Ottery St Mary. Middle: Angel and leaf boss, Northlew. Bottom left: Green Man, Widecombe. Bottom right: Green Man in the porch at Bovey Tracey. Facing page: The Holy Trinity in the porch at Thorverton.

STAINED GLASS

In mediaeval churches, stained glass created what Milton called a "dim religious light", and an atmosphere of mystery and awe. Little of the glass remains in the parish churches of Devon, and that mostly in fragments, such as the beautiful pieces which are to be found at Bere Ferrers, and most especially in the fine set of windows at Doddiscombsleigh. The Reformation swept away most stained glass, believing it to be a distraction. The walls must be white, the windows clear. "Light," wrote the church historian Thomas Fuller, was "God's eldest daughter, and a principall beauty in a building".

The Victorians revived the lost art with enthusiasm, and most of the stained glass to be found in Devon churches is theirs. This has led to the darkening of many Perpendicular buildings which were intended to be chambers of light. The quality of nineteenth-century glass varies enormously, but there are some fine windows, including those by William Morris and Burne-Jones in St John's, Torquay, Clayton & Bell at Dartington, and the wonderful series by Hardman & Co at Kenn. Glowing twentieth-century glass by John Piper and Patrick Reyntiens fills the interior of St Andrew's, Plymouth with rich colours.

15th-century glass at Doddiscombsleigh. Above: Extreme Unction. Facing page: St Christopher.
Page 232: Glass at Axmouth by Bell & Son, c.1890. Page 233: Christ in Glory by Clayton & Bell at Dartington.

SOME REFLECTIONS
ON VISITING CHURCHES

Thoughts about earlier congregations

There are churches which have been Christian sanctuaries for more than a thousand years. And for all that time, they have been not only places where Christ lived sacramentally among his people, places of communal worship and private prayer, but a reminder of our own mortality. At the same time they have always been an expression of community pride and identity. Everything in them bears the imprint of earlier generations.

John Betjeman puts it nicely. "Old glass still diffuses the daylight on the latest hats as softly as it did on the wigs of the eighteenth century or the woollen hose of the people of the Middle Ages. Elizabethan silver is still used for the sacrament. And from the tower a bell, cast soon after the Wars of the Roses, lends its note to the peal that ripples over the meadows and threads its way under the drone of aeroplanes . . . Here lies the England we are all beginning to wish we knew, as the roar of the machine gets louder and the suburbs creep from London to Land's End."

Change in the church

The vicar, like the church in which he or she serves, has not always worn the same vestments, encouraged the singing of the same verses or uttered the same prayers. Likewise changes in ritual have brought about small but significant changes in the placing of fittings. Throughout the centuries, the importance of the chancel, the introduction of altar-rails and box pews, the position of the altar – each a register of the history of different attitudes to worship – have evolved.

The church itself can also have changed. Take, for example, St David's in Exeter: what we see today is the fourth building on or near the present site, each of them dedicated to the same saint. The first was a Chapel of Ease built in 1194. The second was built in 1541 and was twice nearly destroyed, in the Prayer Book Revolt of 1549 and again in the Civil War in 1645. The third, a classical building designed by the architect James Green, was built in 1816. The present church dates from 1897-1900 and has been subject to minor alterations ever since.

Some thoughts about the churches of Devon

Few of Devon's churches are comparable with the greatest parish churches of England, those to be found in, say, Lincolnshire and Norfolk, Suffolk and the Cotswolds. There is probably nothing in the county to rank with St Wendreda in March (Cambridgeshire) with its wonderful winged angels, St Mary Redcliffe in Bristol, with its glorious lierne vaults, or St Patrick in Patrington (Yorkshire) with its tapering spire, rich flowing tracery and flying buttresses.

In spite of the wealth from wool, proudly extravagant buildings are not characteristic of Devon. This is a county of wagon roofs, elaborate rood-screens, pulpits and intricately carved bench ends, but not, one can say, of either austerity or grandiloquence. Grandeur is out of place in the homely Devon landscape, a landscape (on the whole) without elemental contrasts and spectacular effects, one in which the cushiony hillock, the meandering lane, the flower-rich hedgerow and comfortable thatch tend to predominate. The counterpart to our vernal countryside is the lushly carved cornice on a screen entangled with grapes and wild stems.

My friend, Satish Kumar, has drawn attention to the difference between objects, thoughts and actions which are (in Sanskrit) *Sattvic* and those which are *Rajasic*. The former are authentic, ordinary, unassuming and sublime. The latter, are grand and extravagant. With display and decoration, they set out to impress. Employing this ancient Indian concept, I have no doubt as to which of these categories most of the Devon churches belong.

Architecture and light

"Let there be light," said God. And there was light. The fingers of light flickering on plastered walls, the sensuous gleam of paved floors, sunshine blazing through the church's clear panes of glass and defining the edges of a Beer-stone pier – all this is forever transitory.

Visit on a gloomy day and the interior is barely the same place as on a sparkling one. There are other differences too: the lemony brightness of a spring morning little resembles the shadowed darkness of a February afternoon. Snow bleaches the vaults; wind and rain encourage their own grey poetry.

One day, slanting beams of sunlight spotlight the altar as in a painting by Rembrandt. On another day it is as if a Zurbaran was coming to life. The light, firm and powerful, emphasises the three-dimensionality of everything in the building.

The church within a sacred network

We take it for granted that the modern church exists within a network of roads, garages, factories, houses, shops, schools and other secular buildings. How differently we might experience them in a different, a sacred, context.

I saw something of that context in India, where there are not only shrines and temples but places made sacred by worship, pilgrimage and prayer – vermilion-coloured wayside stones, pots hung on the branches of trees, and ash-besmeared mendicants sitting beside a path – all of these acting as a constant reminder of this hidden but ever-present dimension of reality.

Something similar once characterised the mediaeval Devon landscape, sacralised not only by the recurrence of churches, priories and nunneries but other points of access to the holy: shrines, wells, springs, holy crosses, routes of pilgrimage and the sites of martyrdom.

Reflections on changing attitudes to worship

In the early Middle Ages attendance at church was not a matter of choice; it was compulsory. We do not know how many attended weekly mass or fulfilled their obligation of annual communion. Nor do we know how many truly believed in the tenets of the faith, either then or in the sixteenth century. Nonetheless, since Christianity was the matrix of the mediaeval world, the teachings of the Church were accepted as the framework of all human life. They governed birth, marriage, death, sex and eating, made the rules for law and medicine and gave each person their understanding of the cosmic scheme of things, from our origin in the Garden of Eden to their epic conclusion on the Day of Judgement.

Centuries later, the situation had radically changed. In his poem *Dover Beach*, Matthew Arnold foresees how 'The Sea of Faith' once "at the full" would move into withdrawal:

> But now I only hear
> Its melancholy, long, withdrawing roar,
> Retreating, to the breath
> Of the night-wind, down the vast edges drear
> And naked shingles of the world.

By the time this poem was published – in 1867 – Nonconformity was widespread and the numbers who doubted on the increase. The United Kingdom census of 1851 revealed that only half the population regularly attended church. In England between the two World Wars, faith continued its inexorable decline. A recent survey suggests that as many as 55% no longer believe in a higher being.

Reflections on those who built the churches

The names of those who funded the churches of the late mediaeval period, merchants like John Greenway and John Lane, or noblemen and others, like John Evans (a keeper of the Marquis of Dorset's deer park who paid for the fittings at Coldridge), are sometimes recorded. This is especially so when patronage resulted in a permanent feature (such as the Kirkham chantry in St John's, Paignton or the Greenway Chapel in St Peter's, Tiverton), named after the donor.

But the names of the manifold craftsmen who designed and built the churches – the sculptors, glaziers, joiners, carpenters, tilers, painters, woodcarvers, and masons – have remain unrecorded. A few are known – Roger Down and John Hyll at Atherington, and Roger Growdon, who designed the tower of St Mary's, Totnes – but the vast majority are not. Anonymous they may be, yet their work speaks not only of their faith but of their superlative invention and craftsmanship.

The flowering of a rural culture

The churches in Devon's many villages are not only in the country but of the country. Their fabric was made from the trees, the stones, the slates and earth of their immediate locality. Their spirit reflects the landscape.

Prayer

I feel the echo of prayer in these holy places, its fragrance filling their spaces. The prayer of Jean Nicholas Groy (1731-1803), a French Jesuit who fled to England in 1792 comes to me. "Teach us, O God, the silent language which says all things. Teach our souls to remain silent in thy presence, that we may adore thee in the depths of our being and await all things from thee, whilst asking of thee nothing but the accomplishment of thy will. Teach us to remain quiet under thine action and produce in our souls that deep and simple prayer which specifies nothing and expresses everything."

Cranmer

I have been reading Monica Furlong's book on the Church of England, and find her account of the life of Thomas Cranmer of particular interest. He was not only instrumental in the destruction of many decorative features at the Reformation, but the chief compiler of the Protestant prayer books. He wrote with a marvellous economy many of the Collects first published in his Prayer Book. His Collect for Purity opens every communion service:

"Almighty God, unto whom all hearts are open, all desires known, and from whom no secrets are hid: cleanse the thoughts of our hearts by the inspiration of thy Holy Spirit, that we may perfectly love thee, and worthily magnify thy holy Name; through Christ our Lord, Amen."

It was the introduction of Cranmer's Prayer Book which provoked the Prayer Book Rebellion of 1549, begun at Sampford Courtenay and ended at Clyst St Mary with the slaughter of 4,000 rebels. But, as Furlong writes, The Book of Common Prayer and The King James Bible were the founding texts of a culture that was to spread to many parts of the world.

Creativity

How could these small and relatively remote village communities have given birth to such perfect buildings, ones as complex and beautiful as many works of art in our national museums and galleries? Churches such as Ashton, Plymtree or Sutcombe were built to the glory of God, but at the same time, surely, for the satisfaction of the people who made and paid for them. People then, as now, possessed a fierce sense of place that amounted to reverence. The construction of a church enabled them to build bigger and better than a neighbouring village or parish.

But there was, I suggest, another factor behind much mediaeval embellishment – it was a chance for the craftsman to express his creative imagination. We have only to look at the ceiling of the nave at St Andrew's, Cullompton, the bosses in the vaulting at Ottery St Mary, the Decorated-style tracery in the north aisle window at Broadclyst, to see how much the craftsmen of those centuries relished every opportunity to exercise their creative skills.

In his Foreword to *English Parish Churches as Works of Art*, Alec Clifton-Taylor says: "After having, over the past forty years or so, visited several thousand of England's churches, including all the finest, I feel more sure than ever that much of what can be seen came into being as an outcome of the sheer joy of creation, like so much of the best art of every kind the world over. No other explanation need be sought, for no other activity is better worth while."

Wood and stone

My experience of Devon churches is infused by delight in the local materials out of which they have been made: granite, slate, plaster, stone, glass and, pre-eminently, wood. Wood is everywhere: the rood-screens, the vaults, the pulpits, the pews and bench ends, are largely made from it. Devonians have a great gift and passion for wood; hammers, drawknives, chisels, spokeshaves, saws, planes and sandpapers have been their delight. The beauty of it and the other materials out of which these buildings have been made lies in their wildness, their reminder of the natural world of which they are an integral element.

I abhor the employment of all the artificial and suburban things which are creeping into the churches. Examples of what I have in mind can be found in two north Devon churches I have visited recently. In one a wall to wall carpet (red with spots) has been introduced and in the other, very bright red kneelers; both completely out of keeping with the sombre dignity of their venerable interiors.

The Bishop of Salisbury, David Stancliffe, has described this kind of development as the "drawing-room-isation of church buildings". "I am", he says, "for bare stone floors and all those things that make the space actually feel 'other' and different. Because I think that that is actually what is required by the person who steps into this world through the door of the church. It is not just a space that is marked off and characterised by things different from our domestic and organisational life; it is also that that space is somewhere where you can sense encounter." *

The church stripped of richness

For the churchgoer of the pre-Reformation period, the parish church was a place of sensuous mystery. The divine was experienced through the eyes via the church's dazzling artworks and rich sometimes brazen colouring; through the ears through both word and music, and, too, through the sense of smell via the fragrance of incense. With its flickering candles, processions, richness and colour, it was, and is still in some Catholic churches, a theatre of the senses. Visiting today's Anglican churches it is perhaps worth remembering their original nature.

Cells of tranquillity

To visit one of Devon's parish churches is to discover the delicate silence with which they are now enveloped. One sits in peace; only rarely does someone enter and offer a prayer. A Christian church is valued because it offers a sanctuary of peace and quiet.

But how great the contrast with the holy places I experienced in India! Here I remember the noise and bustle of two of its greatest temples: in Madurai, the Minakshi Sundareshvara temple and in Thanjavur, the Brihadishvara temple. Both, from early morning to sunset, were alive with different forms of devotional activity. Hinduism is not in general a congregational activity, its adherents worship singly or in small family groups, but nonetheless the atmosphere can be excited and exciting: bells may be clanging, flame-lit lamps waved, fresh flowers offered and overall there can be the thick sweet smell of incense. The comings and

---

From a paper, 'Churches as Holy Places', given at the Rural Theology Association Conference, which took place at Sarum College in October 1995.

goings of bustling devotees, and the occasional parade in which consecrated processional images of the deities are carried around the temple's lofty spaces, only intensify the devotional atmosphere.

Churchless worship

Reflecting on this book's basic assumption that a building is a necessary component of worship, I have been wondering if that has always been the case.

In Buddhism, the idea of a permanent temple was never a fundamental part of its originator's teaching. The Buddha advised his followers to meditate in the wild: at the roots of a tree, or in a cave, or in any suitable place they could find. He never told them to erect buildings, and he himself attained enlightenment under a wild fig tree.

It is true that Jesus sometimes preached in the Temple, but a similar freedom of approach is to be found in the Gospels. He taught mainly in the open air, and sent his disciples into people's houses. "We look in vain to the New Testament for a detailed building policy," writes Richard Giles. "The main thrust of its teaching lies in relationships and attitudes, rather than bricks and mortar." George Fox, the seventeenth-century founder of the Society of Friends, took a similar attitude. He despised churches – 'steeple houses' he called them – and believed that the Church should be composed of its living members, not of wood and stone. A century later, Charles Wesley also took his faith to the people; he preached in churches while they were open to him, and in the open air when they were not.

The strangeness of the Gothic

Gothic, commonplace in England, is not a style of architecture confined to the ecclesiastical: there are schools, banks, railway stations, and even our Houses of Parliament created in that idiom. Indeed there is so much Gothic that it can be called the vernacular, and as such is often taken for granted, a domestic ordinariness. Some years ago, standing in front of the seven-pointed north porch at St Mary Redcliffe in Bristol, I experienced a surprise, a revelation: for the first time I fully recognised the extraordinary strangeness of the Gothic style. Its luxuriant exoticism was utterly foreign, utterly 'other', yet at the same time paradoxically expressive of the English spirit.

That Englishness, and the rural churches that reflect it, give me a perennial delight. Long may they both continue unendangered.

Facing page: Stowford tower.

Architects and artists
who have worked in Devon

Architects

Edward Ashworth (1815-96) Articled to Robert Cornish of Exeter and then to Charles Fowler. Settled in Exeter in 1846. His church designs and restorations are scholarly but unexciting. Built new churches at Withycombe Raleigh, Lympstone and Topsham, and was responsible for restorations at Cullompton, Tiverton, Bideford, Axminster and Broadclyst,

John Frances Bentley (1839-1902) was the great Catholic architect of Westminster Cathedral. His work in Devon was limited to the fittings of the church at Collaton St ary near Paignton. This includes its polychromatic font, reredos and the stained glass in the chancel.

Sir Arthur Blomfield (1829-99) was a Gothic Revival architect much in demand by the clergy of the Church of England for churches, schools and restorations. Thomas Hardy was in Blomfield's office from 1862-67. In Devon, the latter designed St Luke's in Torquay, and worked with John Hayward on the restoration of Holy Cross, Crediton. Also All Saints, Rackenford.

William Butterfield (1814-1900) Important and prolific High Church architect of the Oxford Movement, a man whose passionate architecture is one of the splendours of the Victorian age. Although he is most famous for All Saints, Margaret Street, London, the chapel of Rugby School and Keble College, Oxford, his work in Devon is especially fine. There is his innovative design for All Saints, Babbacombe (begun in 1865) and the earlier St Bartholomew at Yealmpton (1848). Butterfield was also involved with restorations of Alphington, Abbotskerswell, Morebath and Ottery St Mary, where he designed the font and decorated the south transept.

William Douglas Caröe (1857-1938) entered the London office of J. L. Pearson in 1881, where he worked on the drawings for Truro Cathedral. The experience led to him being appointed as an architect to the Ecclesiastical Commission and, like Temple Moore, a vast amount of church architecture passed through his hands. His principal Devon church, St David's Exeter, was begun in 1897 but he also designed St Sabinus in Woolacombe, St Francis in Sidmouth and St Boniface in Plymouth. Caröe restored St Winifred's at Branscombe and designed the Redvers Buller Memorial at Crediton.

Henry Clutton (1819-93) was a pupil of Edward. Blore and worked with William Burges. He designed various modest Roman Catholic churches in the French Gothic and Romanesque styles including St Peter's, Leamington, St Nicholas, Hatherop in Gloucestershire and St Mary, Woburn in Bedfordshire. In Devon his work was limited to St Mary Magdalene, Tavistock, for the Duke of Bedford.

Charles Fowler (1792-1867) was a pupil of John Powning of Exeter and an assistant to David Laing. In 1818 he set up his own practice. He designed St Paul's in Honiton in the Norman style.

Robert M. Fulford (1845-1910) was articled to Hayward and worked in the offices of William

White. He practised in Exeter and was especially active in the 1880s, but gave up architecture when ordained in 1891. In his restorations he left evidence of a powerful architectural style, as in his work at Poltimore, Washford Pyne and Bow.

E. W. Godwin (1833-86) The architect and designer of the Aesthetic Movement, Godwin became famous for his avant-garde studio houses for artists in Chelsea, including the White House for James McNeil Whistler. His most substantial building is Northampton Town Hall. He was also a designer of furniture, textiles, wallpapers, ceramics and interiors, strongly influenced by Japanese art. In Devon his work was confined to new windows in the churches at Staverton and Littlehempston, designs which have only recently been recognised as his.

Richard Davie Gould (1817-1900) The most significant work of this prolific architect is in Barnstaple where he was Borough Surveyor for 46 years and responsible for several major buildings including the Pannier Market. He was also responsible for the nave and aisle of Down St Mary, the chancel at Sheepwash and the restoration of Winkleigh.

Joseph Aloysius Hansom (1803-82) An important Catholic architect who for a time partnered A. W. Pugin and was also part of a dynasty – he worked with his brother Charles and son Henry John. Hansom designed the classical town hall for Birmingham, founded *The Builder* magazine and invented the Hansom cab. In Devon he was architect of the Roman Catholic Plymouth Cathedral, the Priory at Abbotskerswell and Our Lady, St Marychurch in Torquay.

Rhode Hawkins (1820-84) St Michael, Exeter, with its soaring spire was designed by the little known Rhode Hawkins for William Gibbs of Tyntesfield, Somerset. He also designed St Leonard, a chapel of ease to Bramford Speke,

John Hayward (1808-91) was architect to the Exeter Diocesan Architectural Society from its foundation. His first church, a small chapel at Tipton St John, was built for the Coleridges of Ottery. Another early church, St Andrew, Exwick, was recognised as a forerunner of Camdenian principles. He built new churches at Beer, Bicton, Ilfracombe and Woodbury Salterton, partly rebuilt Uffculme, and restored Holy Cross, Crediton. His most prominent building is the Royal Albert Museum, Exeter.

John James (1672-1746) The son of a parson, John James was a man of some learning. He translated books on architecture and gardening from both Italian and French, and became Nicholas Hawksmoor's fellow surveyor to the Commissioners appointed under the Church-building Act of 1711. Most of his work, of which St George's, Hanover Square, is the best-known example, is in London.

Temple Moore (1856-1920) A pupil of George Gilbert Scott Junior, whose practice he took over in 1890, was a distinguished architect of the Arts and Crafts Movement. His masterpiece is St Wilfred's Harrogate. In Devon, Moore designed the screen at Littleham, near Bideford.

Sir Charles Archibald Nicholson (1867-1949) Articled to J. D. Sedding, of whom he was the true successor. After Sedding's death, Nicholson stayed with Henry Wilson until 1893, when he set up in practice on his own. From 1895-1916 he was in partnership with Major Hubert Christian Corlette, with whom he restored and refitted many existing parish churches and designed about 40 new ones. In Devon Nicholson and Corlette designed St Matthew, Chelston, Torquay and St Paul, Yelverton.

John L. Pearson (1817-98) One of the outstanding Victorian architects, whose most celebrated work includes St Augustine's, Kilburn, St Michael and All Angels, Croydon, and Truro Cathedral. His earliest Devon work is the little church at Landscove. Later, he rebuilt the church at Dartington on a new site, and was also responsible for the restoration of Atherington, Broadhempston, Chagford, Exeter (St Pancras), Swimbridge and Torre (All Saints).

Robert Potter (b. 1909) Inspired by Sir Ninian Comper, he worked mainly as an ecclesiastical architect. His churches include All Saints, Clifton, Bristol, St Aldate's, Gloucester, St Francis, Salisbury, Millmead Church, Guildford, and St Nicholas, Sevenoaks. In Devon he was responsible for one of the county's most distinguished post-war churches, the Church of the Ascension, Crown Hill, Plymouth (1956).

Augustus Welby Northmore Pugin (1812-52) As designer, architect and theorist he was singlehandedly responsible for the early nineteenth-century interpretation of mediaeval art and architecture that blossomed into the Gothic Revival. Pugin designed much of the interior of the Houses of Parliament, several cathedrals and major houses (including his own in Ramsgate), as well as wallpapers, furniture, stained glass and light fittings. In Devon he was responsible for the Mausoleum at Bicton and windows for Dittisham, Upton Pyne and Ottery St Mary.

Anthony Salvin (1799-1881) Pupil of John Nash. Prolific architect of country houses mainly in the Elizabethan and Jacobean style, but also a few churches. In Devon he designed two Torquay churches: St Mark's, Torwood (converted to a theatre) and St Mary Magdalene, Upton. He restored St Nectan's, Ashcombe, while working on Mamhead House, the latter establishing him as the chief architect of his time.

Sir George Gilbert Scott (1811-78), the most prolific of Victorian architects, was to build a multitude of churches, and restore many more. His other works include such iconic buildings as St Pancras Station, the Foreign Office and the Albert Memorial. In Devon his work began with the chapel at Luscombe and continued with major restorations at Barnstaple, Totnes, Fremington and Stowford.

Edmund Harold Sedding (1863-1921) Nephew of John Dando Sedding, the foremost advocate of the theories of the Arts and Crafts Movement. E. H. Sedding did many church restorations, chancel screens and church fittings in Cornwall, Somerset, Suffolk and Essex. In Devon he built St Mary's, Abbotsbury, Newton Abbot, and St Peter's, Shaldon, Teignmouth. He also remodelled St Michael's, Princetown, St James's, Kingston and did restoration work at Broadhempston, Dartmouth, Marwood, Plympton and Sparkwell.

George Edmund Street (1824-81) Street was the original inspiration of the Arts and Crafts Movement: Philip Webb was his assistant and William Morris for a time his pupil. One of the greatest nineteenth-century architects, he built many churches, including Cork Cathedral, but is probably most famous for the Law Courts in the Strand. He was involved with churches in Ashburton, Huish and Down St Mary, but his outstanding work in Devon is St John Evangelist in Torquay.

William Weir (1865-1950) was a leading practitioner and teacher of the methods of restoring old buildings advocated by Philip Webb and William Morris in the 1870s. His major work in Devon was the restoration of Dartington Hall, but he restored churches at Axminster, Crediton, Denbury, Plymtree and Salcombe Regis.

William White (1825-1900) One of the most interesting west-country Gothic Revival architects. He was involved with churches at Hooe, Plymouth, Cadbury, West Down, Clyst Honiton, Upton Pyne, Instow, Landkey, Braunton, Sidmouth, Farringdon, Torrington, Heanton Punchardon and West Anstey.

Other artists and craftsmen

Sir Edward Burne-Jones (1833-98) was one of the painters in the circle round William Morris and Rossetti. As well as paintings he produced many tapestry and stained-glass designs for William Morris's firm. In Devon, his stained glass is to be found at Culmstock, Monkton, Plymouth (Emmanuel) and, especially Torquay (St John Evangelist).

Clayton and Bell (John Richard Clayton, 1827-1913, and Alfred Bell, 1832-95) became partners in 1855, and their stained-glass studio became one of the largest in the Victorian era. In Devon their work is to be found in as many as 36 churches.

Alexander Gibbs (1848-99) came of a family of stained-glass makers. His work is to be found in churches in Bideford, Ottery St Mary, Hemycock, Sidmouth and All Saints, Babbacombe.

John Hardman (1811-67) founded an ecclesiastical metal works at Birmingham in 1838, and in 1844 was persuaded by his friend A.W. N. Pugin to expand the business to include the manufacture of stained glass. Pugin was the chief designer for the firm until his death in 1852. In Devon, Hardman glass is found at Ottery St Mary, Holy Trinity, Ilfracombe, the Mausoleum at Bicton, St John the Evangelist, Plymouth and 26 other churches. There is a particularly fine set of his windows at Kenn.

Harry Hems (1842-1916) Hems arrived in Exeter in 1865 to work on the Royal Albert Memorial Museum, and stayed to establish one of the most prolific ecclesiastical workshops in Victorian England. By the late 1880s he was employing 70 men in Exeter, and staff in London, Oxford and Ireland. The firm's carefully executed Gothic can be seen throughout the county. Excellent screen restoration can be found at Winkleigh, Littleham, Staverton, Kenn and elsewhere.

Charles Eamer Kempe (1837-1907) studied stained glass in the studios of Clayton and Bell. In 1869 he set up his own studio and workshop as an independent designer, and by the turn of the century was employing 50 people. The Kempe workshop produced not only glass but designs for church furniture, screens, altars, vestments, etc. It continued to trade until 1934, having made over 4,000 windows. His signature was a sheaf of corn.

Morris and Co. William Morris (1834-96), artist, poet, novelist, visionary and craftsman, played an important role in the development of Victorian architecture. In 1861 he founded the firm of Morris and Co. which not only went on to produce wallpapers, furniture, tapestries, and stained-glass windows (many designed by Burne-Jones), but a revolution in decorative art. Notable examples of the latter can be found at Torquay (St John), Tavistock (St Eustace), Plymouth (Emmanuel) and Monkton. There are also windows at Butterleigh, Cullompton, Culmstock, Exminster, Okehampton and Withycombe Raleigh.

John Piper (1903-92) Painter, printmaker, photographer, stage designer and stained-glass artist, who in collaboration with the craftsman Patrick Reyntiens produced the great Baptistery Window at Coventry Cathedral, and glass for many other churches, including St Andrew's, Plymouth.

Herbert Read (1860-1950) worked for Hems before establishing his own conservation business in Exeter in 1888. He was responsible for countless restorations of rood-screens, pulpits, lecterns, and much else, not only in Devon. His work can be seen at Ashton, Ashprington, Exbourne, Kenton, Lustleigh and Northlew, as well as in the Cathedral, where the firm made good the bomb damage of 1942.

Glossary of architectural terms

Anglo-Catholic Victorian High Church movement within the Anglican church stressing the Church of England's Catholic continuity.

Apse Semi-circular east end of a chancel or chapel, typically Norman.

Arcade Group of arches on columns or pillars.

Arts and Crafts movement Artistic movement, c.1870-1914, inspired by the writings of John Ruskin and William Morris in response to the development of industrialisation.

Baldacchino Free-standing canopy over altear, supported by columns.

Barrel Roof Continuous round-arched vault.

Bay Vertical unit of a wall or façade; also compartments into which a nave is divided.

Boss Knob or projection, often richly carved, at the intersection of roof vault ribs.

Capital The top of a column or pier.

Celure A canopy over the rood, often decorated with stars.

Chancel Eastern part of a church reserved for the clergy usually containing the choir, sanctuary and main altar.

Chantry Chapel Mediaeval chapel for the celebration of masses, especially for the soul of the founder of the chapel. Usually part of an aisle or small chapel. Suppressed after the Reformation in 1547.

Clerestory Top storey of windows to lighten the nave, commonly inserted in the Perpendicular period but rare in the churches of Devon.

Corbel Stone bracket, usually moulded or carved, often with a human head or an angel.

Crocket Small decorative leafy knob on the outside of an arch mainly used on the outer curve of arches, characteristic of thirteenth- and fourteenth-century Gothic architecture.

Crossing In cruciform churches, the part of the building where, usually under a tower, the nave, chancel and transepts meet.

Cupola Small dome.

Curvilinear Window tracery characterised by curving lines.

Decorated Middle phase of Gothic architecture, characterised by elaborate window tracery, naturalistic carving and ogee arches, c.1250-1350.

Dissenters Members of non-conformist groups who refused to follow the Church of England (or the Roman church) after the Reformation, such as Baptists, Unitarians, Congregationalists and Presbyterians.

Dissolution of the Monasteries Seminal act of the English Reformation initiated by King Henry VIII. Many monastic churches became parish churches.

Early English First phase of Gothic architecture dominant after Norman, characterised by the earliest pointed arches, stiff-leaf carving and simple lancet windows, c.1190-1250.

Easter Sepulchre Recess usually in north wall of chancel where the consecrated bread and wine were kept from Good Friday to Easter Sunday.

Gargoyle Waterspout on the eaves or tower of a church, often carved into fantastic human or animal shapes.

Gothic Architecture Architectural style arriving from France which flourished from about the late twelfth century until the English Reformation in

1540, characterised by the pointed arch.

Gothic Revival Rediscovery by the Victorians of mediaeval Gothic style.

Gothick Eighteenth-century fashion based upon a fanciful interpretation of mediaeval Gothic.

Green Man Sculpted human head with foliage sprouting from his mouth, ears and even eyes. Considered a symbol of fertility.

Hatchments Diamond-shaped boards bearing the coat of arms of a deceased person.

Lancet Narrow pointed window of the Early English period without tracery.

Lantern Small open or glazed structure crowning a dome or a roof.

Lierne *see* Vault.

Middle Ages Period of time traditionally taken to begin with the Norman Conquest (1066). It lasted until either the Tudor victory at Bosworth (1485) or the start of the English Reformation (1534).

Minster Anglo-Saxon missionary community and church, origin of many monasteries and cathedrals.

Mullion Vertical stone divide between glass panes (or lights) of a window.

Nave Main body of the church west of the chancel used by the congregation.

Ogee S-shaped curve, a hallmark of the late Decorated period.

Oxford Movement High Church tendency founded by John Keble and others in 1833 advocating a return to the liturgy of the early Church of England and the architecture of the Middle Ages. A similar movement in Cambridge founded the Camden Society and *The Ecclesiologist* magazine. *See also* Tractarian.

Parclose screen Screen usually of decorative wood between a side chapel and other parts of a church.

Patron Person holding the right to nominate the vicar to a church and normally responsible for the upkeep of the chancel, while the parishioners were responsible for the nave and tower.

Perpendicular Final phase of Gothic architecture, characterised by large windows with panel tracery, flattened arches, impressive towers and fan vaulting, c.1350-1540.

Piscina Recess with basin and drain for washing the sacred vessels.

Plinth Projecting base of a building or a column.

Putti Representation of children, rather like Cupids.

Quatrefoils Ornament in the form of a leaf or flower with four lobes.

Quoins External angle stones.

Rector In the Middle Ages the rector was an independent incumbent who received local tithes and was responsible for the chancel and rectory. A vicar was appointed by a monastic foundation and received lesser tithes. After the Reformation, many monastic livings were transferred to 'lay rectors' who appointed vicars to preach. The distinction is now purely historical.

Reformation In England, the separation of the official church from Roman Catholicism in the 1530s and the adoption of Protestant liturgy.

Reredos Wall or screen behind and above the altar, usually ornamented with a carving or painting.

Rib Projecting feature of a vault which is sometimes ornamental, often structural.

Rood Cross Crucifixion group of Christ flanked by the Virgin and St John, usually carved but sometimes painted, above the screen dividing the chancel from the nave. The screen carried a loft in which singers and musicians would perform the Easter Week rituals, and its wainscot was often painted with saints or sybils. The rood-screen is common in the churches of Devon, and although many were removed during the Reformation. 140 have survived in Devon.

Royal Arms Arms of the monarch usually painted on wood or canvas but sometimes carved. Compulsory in churches after the Reformation.

Sanctuary Most sacred part of the chapel, around the altar and associated with the rituals of the Mass.

Sedilia Recessed seats (usually three) in the south wall of the chancel for the priest, deacon and sub-deacon who officiated in the High Mass.

Spandrel Spaces between arches, roughly triangular in shape.

Sgraffito A technique using a scratching effect on wall plaster.

Tester Flat canopy over a pulpit, also called a sounding board.

Tracery Ornamental stone ribs in the upper parts of windows and in circular windows.

Tractarian Relating to the High Church or Ango-Catholic Oxford Movement, resulting from the publication of 90 tracts published in Oxford 1833-41.

Transepts The arms projecting north and south from the crossing of a cruciform church.

Tympanum Space between the lintel and arch of a doorway or opening.

Vault Stone roof. A barrel vault (also called a tunnel or, if ceiled, a wagon roof) comprises a simple semi-circular roof running the length of a nave or aisle or chancel. A rib is a projecting feature of a vault, sometimes structural and sometimes decorative. Tierceron ribs rise from supporting piers to the vault apex, but do not cross other ribs. Lierne ribs join and cross other ribs and do not rise from piers.

Fourteenth-century tiles, Haccombe.

Bibliography

I could not have written this book without an intensive reading of writers whose books about the county's parish churches have been an inspiration and example. In particular I would like to mention J. M. Slader's *The Churches of Devon*, a pioneering study concluding with a comprehensive appendix detailing everything from bench ends to windows. But it was published in 1968 and is long out of print. I also relied on W. G. Hoskins's *Devon* (1954) which contains sensitive and helpful descriptions of every church in the county. It is also outstandingly good on the history, landscape and economy of Devon. Then, of course, there is Nikolaus Pevsner's vast and scholarly contribution to the appreciation of English architecture, which includes his *Devon* in the Buildings of England series (first published in 1952 and revised by Bridget Cherry in 1991), an indispensable resource. Other volumes to which I feel a debt are John Betjeman's *English Parish Churches*, which in its first edition of 1958 lists 77 Devon churches (and 122 in its second, fatter 1993 edition), Anne Jellicoe's *Shell Guide to Devon* (1975) and Simon Jenkins' *England's Thousand Best Churches* (1999), which have also been invaluable sources of information and insight. Although I barely referred to it, I was also aware of Michael Salter's *The Old Parish Churches of Devon*, published in 1999.

I am also grateful to those who wrote the guidebooks to individual churches, which are generally available in most of them.

Devon

Frederick Bligh Bond and Dom Bede Camm, *Roodscreens and Roodlofts*, Sir Isaac Pitman & Sons, 1909.

C. J. P. Cave, *Medieval carvings in Exeter Cathedral*, Penguin Books, 1953.

Bridget Cherry and Nikolaus Pevsner, *The Buildings of England: Devon*, Penguin Books, 1991.

Eamon Duffy, *The Voices of Morebath: Reformation & Rebellion in an English Village*, Yale University Press, 2001.

Helen Harris, *A Handbook of Devon Parishes: A Complete Guide*, Halsgrove, 2004.

W. G. Hoskins, *Devon*, Collins, 1964 & Phillimore & Co. Ltd. 2003.

Walter Jacobson, *Around the Churches of Exeter*, 1998.

Ann Jellicoe & Roger Mayne, *Devon: A Shell Guide*, Faber & Faber, 1975.

Simon Jenkins, *England's Thousand Best Churches*, Allen Lane, The Penguin Press, 1999.

Laurence Jones, *The Beauty of English Churches*, Constable, 1971.

Nigel Kerr, ed., *Sir John Betjeman's Guide to English Parish Churches*, HarperCollins, 1993.

John Lane, *In Praise of Devon*, Green Books, 1998.

William Lock, H. Martin Stuchfield & William

Hemore, *The Monumental Brasses of Devon*, Monumental Brass Society, 2000.

G. Oliver, *Ecclesiastical Antiquities of Devon* (3 volumes), 1840-2.

Nicholas Orme, *Unity and Variety: A History of the Church in Devon and Cornwall*, University of Exeter Press, 1991.

Thomas Packenham, *Meetings with Remarkable Trees*, Weidenfeld & Nicolson, 1996.

W. H. H. Rogers, *The Ancient Sepulchral Effigies of Devon*, 1877.

Michael Salter, *The Old Parish Churches of Devon*, Folly Publications, 1999.

John Scott, James Clarke and Frank Mack, *Towers and Bells of Devon* (two volumes), Mint Press, 2006.

J. M. Slader, *The Churches of Devon*, David & Charles, 1968.

W. Spreat, *Picturesque Sketches of the Churches of Devon*, 1832.

David Spurr, *Devon Churches* (2 small volumes), Merlin Books Ltd, 1984.

John Stabb, *Some Old Devon Churches* (3 volumes), 1909-16.

Christopher Stell, *An Inventory of Nonconformist Chapels and Meeting Houses in South-West England*, HMSO, 1991.

General

Lucy Archer, *Architecture in Britain & Ireland 600-1500*, The Harvill Press, 1999.

John Baker, *English Stained Glass of the Medieval Period*, Thames and Hudson, 1978.

John Betjeman, *In Praise of Churches*, John Murray, 1996.

Frederick Burgess, *English Churchyard Memorials*, 1963.

Wesley Carr et al., *Say One for Me: The Church of England in the Next Decade*, SPCK, 1992.

C. J. P. Cave, *Roof Bosses in Mediaeval Churches*, Cambridge University Press, 1948.

Mark Chatfield, *Churches the Victorians Forgot*, Moorland Publishing, 1979.

Alec Clifton-Taylor, *English Parish Churches as Works of Art*, B. T. Batsford, 1974.

Nicola Coldstream, *The Decorated Style of Architecture and Ornament 1240-1360*, British Museum Press, 1994.

G. Cook, *The English Medieval Parish Church*, Phoenix House, 1954.

Olive Cook, John Hutton and Edwin Smith, *English Parish Churches*, Thames & Hudson, 1971.

F. H. Crossley, *English Church Craftsmanship*, B. T. Batsford, 1941.

C. S. L. Davies, *Peace, Print & Protestantism 1450-1558*, Fontana Press, 1995.

Eamon Duffy, *The Stripping of the Altars: Traditional Religion in England c.1400-1580*, Yale University Press, 1992.

Katherine A. Esdaile, *English Church Monuments 1510-1840*, Oxford University Press, 1946.

Clive Fewins, *The Church Explorer's Handbook*, Canterbury Press, 2005.

Matthew Fox, *A New Reformation: Creation Spirituality and the Transformation of Christianity*, Inner Traditions, 2006.

Stephen Friar, *A Companion to the English Parish Church*, Alan Sutton Publishing Ltd, 1996.

Monica Furlong, *C of E: The State It's In*, Hodder & Stoughton, 2000.

Richard Giles, *Re-Pitching the Tent*, Canterbury Press, 1997.

Robin Gill, *The Myth of the Empty Church*, SPCK, 1993.

Francesca Greenoak, *God's Acre*, W. I. Books Ltd, 1985.

Martin Harrison, *Victorian Stained Glass*, Barrie and Jenkins, 1980.

Robert Harrison, *The Daily Telegraph Guide to England's Parish Churches*, Aurum Press, 2006.

John Harvey, *The Perpendicular Style*, B. T. Batsford, 1978.

Clive Hicks, *The Green Man: A Field Guide*, Compass Books.

Rosemary Hill, *God's Architect: Pugin and the Building of Romantic Britain*, Allen Lane, 2007.

Peter Howell and Ian Sutton, *The Faber Guide to Victorian Churches*, Faber and Faber, 1989.

Lawrence Jones, *The Beauty of English Churches*, Constable, 1978.

Richard Kiechkhefer, *Theology in Stone: Church Architecture from Byzantium to Berkeley*, Oxford University Press, 2004.

Christopher Martin, *A Glimpse of Heaven: Catholic Churches of England and Wales*, English Heritage, 2006.

Thomas Moore, *The Soul's Religion*, Bantam, 2003.

Richard Morris, *Churches in the Landscape*, J. M. Dent & Sons, 1989.

Colin Platt, *The Parish Churches of Medieval England*, Secker and Warburg, 1981.

John Martin Robinson, *Treasures of the English Churches*, Sinclair-Stevenson, 1995.

Roger Scruton, *The English Tradition in England: an Elegy*, Chatto & Windus, 2000.

Paul Thompson, *William Butterfield*, Routledge & Kegan Paul, 1971.

Marcus Whiffen, *Stuart and Georgian Churches outside London 1603-1837*, B. T. Batsford, 1947.

Further Information

Devon Historic Churches Trust, PO Box 55, Newton Abbot, Devon TQ12 2EG. A registered charity, set up in 1972 to raise funds for the repair and preservation of places of worships of all denominations throughout Devon.

The Historic Churches Preservation Trust, 31 Newbury Street, London EC1A 7HU. (Tel. 020 7600 6090). Founded in 1953, this is the national charity offering funds to communities for essential repairs to the fabric of Christian churches and chapels in England and Wales, regardless of denomination and grade. It receives no direct financial assistance from either the government or the church authorities, and survives entirely on voluntary contributions. At the present time it protects over 300 churches.

The Churches Conservation Trust, 1 West Smithfield, London EC1A 9EE (Tel. 020 7213 0660). This is the national body that cares for and preserves English churches of historic, architectural or archaeological importance that are no longer needed for regular worship. There are currently 338 Trust churches scattered widely throughout England, all of them welcome to visitors and maintained in good repair. In Devon the Trust takes responsibility for ten remarkable churches: in Bradstone, Exeter (St Martin's), Luffincott, North Huish, Parracombe, Princetown, Revelstoke, Satterleigh, Torbryan and West Ogwell.

Ancient Monuments Society and Friends of Friendless Churches, St Anne's Vestry Hall, 2 Church Entry, London EC4V 5HB (Tel: 020 7236 3934). These two conservation societies work in close partnership. The latter was founded in 1957 to save disused but beautiful old places of worship from destruction and ruin; it is directly responsible for over thirty such buildings in England and Wales. Two of these – Ayshford Chapel and South Huish, near Kingsbridge – are in Devon.

Index